CALVIN
An Introduction to His Thought

T. H. L. Parker

 WESTMINSTER/JOHN KNOX PRESS
Louisville, Kentucky

© T.H.L. Parker 1995

First published 1995
by Geoffrey Chapman
a Cassell imprint
Wellington House, 125 Strand, London WC2R.0BB

Published in the U.S.A. by Westminster John Knox Press
100 Witherspoon Street, Louisville, Kentucky 40202-1396

First American Edition

PRINTED IN GREAT BRITAIN

95 96 97 98 99 00 01 02 03 04 – 10 9 8 7 6 5 4 3 2 1

Library of Congress Cataloging-in-Publication Data

Parker, T. H. L. (Thomas Henry Louis), date.
  Calvin : an introduction to his thought / T.H.L. Parker. –
1st American ed.
      p.   cm.
  Includes bibliographical references.
  ISBN 0–664–25602–3 (pbk)
  1. Calvin, Jean, 1509–1564.   2. Theology, Doctrinal–History–16th
century.   I. Title.
  BX9418.P33 1995
  230'.42'092–dc20   95–1055

Contents

I intended only to give some elementary teaching by which anyone who had been touched by an interest in religion might be formed to true godliness. And I was especially diligent in this work for the sake of our own people of France. I saw very many of them hungering and thirsting for Christ but very few who were imbued with even a slight knowledge of him. That this is what I proposed the book itself bears witness by its simple and even rudimentary form of teaching.

John Calvin, Institutio (1536 edition)

My intention in this work has been so to prepare and train aspirants after sacred theology in reading the Divine Word that they may have an easy access into it and then proceed in it without stumbling. For I think I have so embraced the sum of religion in all its parts and arranged it in order that anyone who grasps it aright will have no difficulty in determining both what he ought especially to look for in Scripture and to what end he should refer everything contained in Scripture. Thus I have, as it were, paved the way . . .

John Calvin, Institutio (1539 edition)

In the first edition of this work of ours I did not in the least expect that success which, out of his infinite goodness, the Lord has given. Thus, for the most part I treated the subject summarily, as is usually done in small works. But when I realized that it was received by almost all godly men with a favor for which I never would have ventured to wish, much less to hope, I deeply felt that I was much more favored than I deserved. Consequently I thought that I should be showing extreme ingratitude not to try at least, to the best of my slender ability, to respond to this warm appreciation for me, an appreciation that demanded my further diligence. Not only did I attempt this in the second edition, but each time the work has been reprinted since then, it has been enriched with some additions. Although I did not regret the labor spent, I was never satisfied until the work had been arranged in the order now set forth. Now I trust that I have provided something that all of you will approve.

John Calvin, Institutio (1559 edition)

Preface

In Calvin's *Institutio* is concentrated and ordered the teaching found throughout his sermons and commentaries, his occasional pieces and letters. Although I cannot agree with those who have called him 'a man of one book', yet I freely accept that the *Institutio* comprehends the whole of his thought. Here we may learn why he seceded from Rome, why he strove to reform the Church, and what was the shape of his reforms. We may perceive in this mirror of his mind his view of the world and its history, his understanding of contemporary Europe, the dangers threatening it, his fears for its future. Above all we can hear a declaration of faith, direct and simple save where controversy forces him into involved debate.

If, therefore, we wish to describe Calvin in the context of outstanding Christian thinkers we cannot do better than expound the *Institutio*, assured that its comprehensiveness will be reflected, even in miniature, in our exposition. More, I have tried not only to reflect the comprehensiveness but also to be guided in his every chapter and every paragraph by Calvin's own expressed intentions (see pp. 9–10). This may seem too obvious a method to mention, but I have yet to find any previous expositor of Calvin's thought as a whole who has adopted it as his deliberate programme.

Suggestions for further reading will be given in the notes. For the multitudinous literature on Calvin bibliographies should be consulted: W. Niesel, *Calvin-Bibliographie 1901–1959* (Munich, 1961); D. Kempff, *A Bibliography of Calviniana 1959–1974* (Leiden, 1975); and P. De Klerk's annual bibliography in *Calvin Theological Journal*.

Quotations from the *Institutio* will be given in the following form: the Book number (in roman capitals) followed by the chapter number (in roman lower case) followed by the paragraph number (in arabic numerals); then the *Opera Selecta* reference, with the volume in roman capitals followed by the page number in arabic and the line numbers above. Thus xvi.1, 187[19–21], means in this case Book I, chapter xvi, paragraph 1, to be found in lines 19–21 of p. 187 of, in this case, Vol. I of *Opera Selecta*. (The Book number and the *Opera Selecta* volume are given only at the beginning of each Book or in cross-references.)

Opera Selecta is abbreviated as OS; *Calvini Opera* (in *Corpus Reformatorum*) as CO.

I should like to thank Brian Davies, OP, first for encouraging me to write and then for the many improvements he has suggested. I am grateful also to the publishers for all the helpfulness and patience they have shown.

T.H.L. Parker

Cambridge

Introduction

1 CALVIN'S WRITINGS

Calvin was in the second wave of Reformers. By the time he was born (1509) in north-eastern France, Luther was a grown man, Erasmus already laying out new paths in New Testament studies. He was still a schoolboy when Luther issued his challenge of the Ninety-Five Theses in 1517. The battle lines were being drawn up while he was an arts student in the University of Paris. Rome, Wittenberg, and Zürich had taken up their settled positions before he himself began to worry about the problems raised; after many doubts and hesitations, he sided with Luther.[1]

The date of this conversion is disputed. Perhaps it was while he was studying law at Orléans and Bourges; not impossibly even earlier in his Paris days. What is certain is that when he had become a tutor in one of the Paris colleges he was mixing in reformist circles and was soon to be implicated in the composition of a university rectorial address adjudged heretical by the Faculty of Theology. After some months in hiding he was forced to leave France. He spent a year in Basel, during which he completed and published (1536) the first edition of his *Christianae Religionis Institutio*, 'The Principles of the Christian Religion'. A brief spell in Italy as a secretary to the Duchess of Ferrara was followed by the very different career of biblical lecturer and pastor. in the newly reformed Geneva. This was to be his home for the rest of his life, apart from a period (1538–41) as pastor of the French Church in Strasbourg.

He revised and greatly enlarged the *Institutio* for an edition of 1539 and translated it into French in 1541. This second recension held its place for eighteen years, with some changes and refinements in 1543 and 1550. It was again totally rearranged and augmented for the definitive edition, appearing in 1559 in the form in which we now know it.

His ministry in Geneva provided the impetus for most of his other literary work. In the 59 quarto double-columned volumes of his *opera omnia* in *Corpus Reformatorum*, the *Institutio* in its several recensions occupies only four. A further five or six suffice for occasional writings and another eleven for correspondence. Of the rest, no fewer than 35 volumes are needed to accommodate his biblical works. These are the commentaries, probably based on lectures, on all the New Testament except 2 and 3 John and Revelation, and on the Pentateuch, Joshua, Psalms and Isaiah.[2] To these must be added verbatim transcripts of his lectures on all the Prophets and verbatim transcripts of sermons in which he preached verse by verse through Genesis, Deuteronomy, Judges, 1 and 2 Samuel, Job, nearly all the Prophets, some Psalms, part of a harmony of the Gospels, Acts, 1 and 2 Corinthians, Galatians, Ephesians, 1 and 2 Thessalonians, the Pastoral Epistles and Hebrews.[3]

We must, for reasons of space, confine ourselves in this book to the exposition of one work, the *Institutio*. But we must not forget that its author is this man of diverse parts – the dogmatic theologian, the biblical scholar, the pastor, the ecclesiastical reformer – who has exercised a wide influence in the Church, in political and social economy, and in literature.

2 THE CONTEMPORARY SCENE

The *Institutio* was written in and for the sixteenth century. It was directed to sixteenth-century readers with sixteenth-century patterns of thought. Thus it was given its distinctive ethos by the need to address contemporary institutions and intellectual and moral movements.

First, the Rome from which the Reformers seceded, Rome before and newly through the Council of Trent. 'Rome' is a broad concept. There is no comprehensive standpoint which would have been accepted both by the obscurantists who could call the Greek New Testament a heretical book and also by those who entered into sensible dialogue with the Reformers. A common allegiance to the institution of the Papacy and to general tenets bonded together the disparate movements of Thomists, Augustinians, Occamists, Scotists and, soon, Jesuits. Calvin's polemic does not always cover them all at the same time. His customary terms are 'Papists' (generally the contemporary Romanists), 'Scholastics' and 'Sophists', the first of which refers to mediaeval theologians, the latter to both mediaeval and contemporary. 'Sorbonnists' denotes the obscurantist Paris Faculty.

With the schoolmen he makes a distinction between the better, of an earlier period, and the progressively degenerate of the later. The Church fathers (with whom we may include Bernard of Clairvaux) are in an altogether different class.[4] Despite some weaknesses and aberrations they are usually 'those holy men' on whom Calvin will rely for confirmation, and to whom he will direct the reader as saying this or that better than he could say it himself. Most frequently quoted is Augustine, usually with approval. Others will appear at special places – Hilary of Poitiers on Christology, or Cyprian on the Church, for example.

Where to place the heart of the Reformers' dissent from Rome is far from easy. Possibly it was their insistence on the supremacy of grace over sin, although this itself may suggest different concepts of the work of the Mediator. Calvin himself saw it in different attitudes to Scripture. If the Romanists would agree with us on 'Scripture alone' he said, all the other questions would speedily be settled.

Secondly, there were the Anabaptists, whom Calvin calls sometimes by that name, sometimes 'fanatics', sometimes 'enthusiasts', sometimes 'libertines'.[5] Here again there was not one well-defined body but a large number of anti-Roman, anti-Establishment groups with differing, often opposed, views. At the one extreme the more conservative Anabaptists were not far removed from left-wing Reformers, apart from their rebaptizing and refusal to baptize infants. At the other extreme stood the anarchists, the exponents of free love, and the Trinitarian heretics. We shall meet with most of them on our journey.

Thirdly, the humanists. In this term are included not simply those who knew Greek and Hebrew, who respected the civilization of Greece and Rome, who cultivated an Augustan style in their own writing and who took an informed interest in the scientific discoveries that were beginning to be made. The typical Renaissance humanist went further than this. As P. O. Kristeller put it, 'the core and center of Renaissance humanism' is 'the emphasis on the Greek and Latin classics as the chief subjects of study and as unrivalled models of imitation in writing and in thinking and even in actual conduct'.[6]

Caution must be used when considering Calvin's relation to humanism.[7] Taking Kristeller's definition, did Calvin regard the classics as 'the chief subjects' of his study? If so, was he self-deceived in claiming (as he often did) the Bible as his chief subject? Again, did he regard the classics as 'unrivalled models of imitation . . . in thinking and even in actual conduct'? If so, why does he give the primacy to the Law and the Gospel? It would be better if those who are so eager to make Calvin a humanist *tout court* were to consider all the evidence of his career and writings, and at least to admit a few qualifications. This much, however, may safely be said. He had a deep affection for, and a wide knowledge of, the classical authors; he wrote good Augustan prose; he adopted the rhetoric of Aristotle, Cicero and Quintilian; he used various classical philosophies like Stoicism and Platonism; finally, he, like any other man, was not so in control of all his thinking as always to eradicate all extra-biblical ideas from his mind, even though his aim avowedly was to be so true to Scripture as not to swerve 'a nail's breadth' from its teaching.

Lastly, the extreme humanists, especially the free-thinkers in Paris – Rabelais, Dolet, des Périers and the other Epicurean devotees of a neo-paganism. This movement filled Calvin with alarm as the most dangerous of all threats to European society. When, as so often, in the *Institutio* we come upon attacks on the Epicureans it is usually of this group that we should think.

3 THE INTERPRETATION OF THE *INSTITUTIO*

The *Institutio* developed from six chapters in 1536 through the seventeen of 1539 and the 21 of 1543–50 to the four Books of 1559. Our task now is to describe the character of these recensions and thus to learn how the work should be interpreted.

The first edition was framed on the lines of traditional catechisms or primers, which had aimed at teaching young Christians the elements of the Christian Faith. They commonly consisted of instruction on the Apostles' Creed, the Ten Commandments and the Lord's Prayer. To these was added in the Reformation period teaching on the Sacraments. The 1536 *Institutio*, following this pattern, contained chapters on the Law, the Faith, and Prayer (with expositions on the Commandments, the Creed and the Lord's Prayer respectively), as well as chapters on the Sacraments and a threefold final chapter on Christian liberty, the authority of the Church and political authority.

The form reflected Calvin's intention in writing the book. In the Letter to the King of France which prefaced this edition (and was retained in all subsequent editions) he explained his purpose. At the outset, he said, he had not planned an *apologia* for Church reform: 'I intended only to give some elementary teaching by which anyone who had been touched by an interest in religion might be formed to true godliness. And I was especially diligent in this work for the sake of our own people of France. I saw very many of them hungering and thirsting for Christ but very few who were imbued with even a slight knowledge of him. That this is what I proposed the book itself bears witness by its simple and even rudimentary form of teaching' (OS I.21). It was only when the book was completed or nearing completion that Calvin saw that the work would also serve as an explanation to the King and his advisers of the real beliefs of the French Reformers, who were far from being, as they were now represented, Anabaptists and heretics. The apologetic character of the book was therefore incidental; its essential character was catechetical, to give elementary teaching to those who had begun to be interested in the Faith, to those who were 'hungering and thirsting for Christ'.

Within a little while Calvin became dissatisfied with his *Institutio* and set out to revise it. The new edition was three times the length of the first. Moreover, the catechetical form had been dropped in favour of a systematic arrangement of the main doctrines (as Calvin saw them) of Holy Scripture. These are, following his chapters: The knowledge of God / The knowledge of man and free-will / The Law (with an exposition of the Decalogue) / The Faith (with an exposition of the Apostles' Creed) / Penitence / Justification by faith and the merits of works / The likeness and differences between the Old and New Testaments / Predestination and God's Providence / Prayer (with an exposition of the Lord's Prayer) / The Sacraments / Baptism / The Lord's Supper / Christian liberty / The authority of the Church / Political authority / The five 'falsely-named' sacraments / The life of a Christian man.

In 1543 were added chapters on Vows and on Human traditions; and to the chapter on the Faith three others in which the Creed was

5

expounded more thoroughly. There is also some rearrangement of the order of chapters. The final form of this recension (1550) tidied up several mistakes, enlarged two or three chapters, and gave added clarity to the paragraphs by numbering them.

A prefatory address to the reader in 1539 and a summary of the contents in 1543 explain why the revision had been made and in what the character of this group of editions consists. As he discloses his purpose we see that a change has taken place in the readership for which the book was chiefly intended, and correspondingly a change in the form of the book itself: 'My intention in this work has been so to prepare and train aspirants after sacred theology [i.e., theological students] in reading the Divine Word that they may have an easy access into it and then proceed in it without stumbling' (CO 1, 255[6]). 'Those who have been touched by an interest in religion' and 'those who are hungering and thirsting for Christ' are certainly not excluded from the number of 'aspirants after sacred theology'; but the new category implies a change of tone from helping on babes in the Faith to instructing the more mature. The first edition did not here mention Holy Scripture; no doubt it was taken for granted. But now Scripture is put in the foreground. The 1539–50 *Institutio*, to use Calvin's terms of rhetoric, opens the door into the reading and understanding of Scripture and thereafter smooths the path of further understanding.

Concurrently with the revising of the *Institutio* was being written the first-fruits of the New Testament commentaries, *Romans*. It was his grappling with the problem of the form of his commentary that determined also the form of the revised *Institutio*. New Testament exposition had traditionally followed one of the two ways of exegesis: either of individual words and phrases or interpretation of the general meaning of passages. The mediaeval expositor, in his written commentaries and even more in his lectures, had concentrated on the former. Fifteenth- and early sixteenth-century Renaissance writers, however, preferred to give a more general interpretation. In particular it was seen that Aristotle and, for the Latins, Cicero had advocated the method by which the more important subjects in a passage were extracted and written up as separate articles. These more important subjects were called by Aristotle 'topics' or 'places' (*topoi*; in Cicero *loci*). Those which were gathered out of a whole book or the complete Bible and, therefore, were common to the whole were called 'common places' (*loci communes*).[8]

Melanchthon was the first to apply this method to the New Testament and he was quickly followed by others, notably, for our present argument, by Martin Bucer. When Calvin embarked on his career as New Testament commentator he had, therefore, to choose between the methods. He knew Melanchthon's work and also Bucer's commentary on Romans, which came out in the same month as the 1536 *Institutio*. In the event neither Melanchthon nor Bucer won his complete approval. Melanchthon's commentary largely neglected detailed exegesis in favour of theological exposition. Bucer supplied abundant exegesis as well as very long doctrinal treatises (*loci communes*), all of which, put together within one volume, made the work so lengthy as to be virtually unreadable. In one respect, however, they showed Calvin the way forward. It would be possible to write a commentary in the time-honoured way of straight exposition with its attendant exegesis, and to assemble the *loci communes* in a separate book as Melanchthon had done with his *Loci communes rerum theologicarum* (1521). This separate book became the second edition of the *Institutio*.

We return to the address to the reader:

My intention in this work has been so to prepare and train aspirants after sacred theology in reading the Divine Word that they may have an easy access into it and then proceed in it without stumbling. For I think I have so embraced the sum of religion in all its parts and arranged it in order that anyone who grasps it aright will have no difficulty in determining both what he ought especially to look for in Scripture and to what end he should refer everything contained in Scripture. Thus I have, as it were, paved the way; and if in the future I publish any commentaries on Scripture I shall always condense them and keep them short, for I shall have no need to undertake lengthy doctrinal discussions or digress into *loci communes*. In this way the godly reader will be spared much trouble and tedium, provided he approaches [the commentaries] fore-armed with a knowledge of the present work as a necessary instrument. But because my commentary on the Epistle to the Romans will furnish an example of this intention, I prefer to let it speak for itself rather than forecast it by my words now. (CO 1, 255/6)

This recension of the *Institutio*, therefore, is tied firmly not only to Scripture but also to the author's commentaries on Scripture. Had Calvin been Bucer, most of the material in the 1539 *Institutio* would now be found scattered throughout his commentary on Romans. If the first edition was the 'catechetical' *Institutio*, the second might be called the 'topical' *Institutio*, the *Institutio* of the *topoi*, the *loci communes*. Nevertheless, he has taken the care to arrange the *loci* in an order that should correspond to the Faith of Scripture. He can even speak of this aggregation as constituting a *summa religionis*, a comprehensive statement of the Christian religion.

The four chapters of 1539–50 expounding the Apostles' Creed now dictate the shape of the whole work. Calvin divided the Creed into four parts, not the usual three:

(1) I believe in God the Father almighty, Maker of heaven and earth;
(2) I believe in Jesus Christ his only Son our Lord;
(3) I believe in the Holy Spirit;
(4) I believe the holy catholic Church.

Under these four heads the *loci communes* of the earlier version are rearranged, often rewritten, often added to, giving us at last four Books:

Book I: On the Knowledge of God the Creator.
Book II: On the Knowledge of God the Redeemer in Christ, which was revealed first to the Fathers under the Law and then also to us in the Gospel.
Book III: On the Way the Grace of Christ is to be received; what Fruits come to us from it and what Effects follow.
Book IV: On the external Means or Helps by which God invites us into the Society of Christ and keeps us in it.

This edition of the *Institutio* is not, however, a direct exposition of the Creed. Only rarely (as Book II, ch. xvi) does it become this. Nor are there chapters devoted specially to its exposition, like ch. iv in 1539, v–viii in 1543. But even when the Creed is not visible, we should bear it in mind as a character waiting in the wings. What is more, the order of topics in the Creed is not strictly kept. 'The forgiveness of sins' comes in Book III, ch. xiv, and 'the resurrection of the body' in ch. xxv of that Book. Yet the place of the Creed in the *Institutio* is not purely formal. It determines the understanding and interpretation of the work. We may therefore complete our labelling of the recensions by calling this the 'credal' *Institutio*.

In the description of the shape of the *Institutio* we have also been given the clues to its character. The doctrines which go to make up the work are no longer a set of *loci communes* selected and arranged by a private theologian. They now claim for themselves the reflected authority of the oldest working Creed in Christendom, the Creed assented to by the Orthodox, the Roman Catholics, the Lutherans, the Reformed and the Church of England. It should go without saying that this in no way implies a move away from Scripture towards 'Church tradition'. Calvin's position on the authority of Scripture remained the same, as is evidenced by the fact that the rest of the address to the reader is left unchanged from 1539. But it does suggest that by the new form of the *Institutio* Calvin is claiming that its teaching is an authentic statement of the Faith of the one, holy, catholic and apostolic Church. More than that, however (and this is surely Calvin's chief reason for the manner of the revision), the Trinitarian form accorded more clearly and strongly with the character of his theology, which had been Trinitarian from the beginning. The very form is used to declare the unity and the threefoldness of the Godhead. As the first three Books correspond to the credal witness to Father, Son and Holy Spirit, so, but less obviously, the titles of these Books testify to the unity by speaking only of 'God' and not of 'Father', 'Son', or 'Holy Spirit'.

The interpretation of the *Institutio*, then, must be governed by its form. This may be a literary truism, but the misunderstandings of the work and, therefore, of Calvin's theology have more often than not been accompanied by a wrenching of its form into one that fitted the misinterpretation. A blatant example was the thesis that Calvin was mistaken in casting the *Institutio* in four Books, since it should rather be divided into two, on the knowledge of God the Creator and on the knowledge of God the Redeemer.

But Calvin goes out of his way to make everything plain and straightforward for his readers. First, he has arranged the work in four Books. We accept the fact and let it guide our thinking. Each Book is given a precise title – that is, one which accurately declares its contents. Each Book is divided into chapters which are also clearly labelled. Each chapter is divided into paragraphs, connected and separated by numbering. Now, all the titles are what we may call Calvin's stage-directions, informing us of the 'location' and of the 'characters' we shall hear speaking. There is a letter from Edwyn Bevan to Robert Bridges (anent the agèd Poet Laureate's wrestling with *The Testament of Beauty*) which is relevant here: 'It was the practice of the ancients in long poems to give these indications regularly. They began by stating the subject of the poem as a whole . . . and one finds them before each section, saying what it is going to be about.'[9] This is precisely Calvin's practice in the *Institutio*. Not only does he carefully label each Book and each chapter, but he also links up Book with Book, chapter with chapter. Book II, ch. ii provides a clear example: 'Now that we have seen that . . . it remains to examine more closely whether . . . But the truth of this question will dawn on us more easily if I first set out the end to which the whole sum of the matter is to be directed.' What more could we ask? To follow strictly Calvin's stage-directions, as this book sets out to do, must be regarded as indispensable to the correct interpretation of his theology. And how carefully he wrote was noted by the first English translator of the *Institutio*, Thomas Norton:

> At my said first edition of this booke I considered how the Author thereof had of long time purposely laboured to write the same most exactly, and to packe great plenty of matter in small roome of words, yea, and those so circumspectly and precisely ordered . . . that the sentences were thereby become so full; as nothing might well be added without idle superfluity, and againe so nicely pared, that nothing could be minished without taking away some necessary substance of matter therein expressed.[10]

This concise style of the *Institutio*, however hard it makes the translator's task, is in fact a help to readers, so long as they are prepared to attend closely to what is said. On the other hand, we must not give the impression that it reads like an algebra textbook, with problems that move from statement to resolution coolly and disinterestedly. Those who have spoken of its 'remorseless logic' or lack of passion seem to have been reading a different *Institutio* from the one I possess. Readers must judge for themselves in what follows whether the quotations are passionless, detached from life, coldly cerebral, or whether they are not rather warm, pastoral, sometimes homely, often angry, satirical. Notice how often, instead of the impersonal 'man' or 'he', Calvin falls into direct address with the second person singular, how almost universally he uses the first person plural, just as in his sermons. Unless we remember that the *Institutio* was written for those 'hungering and thirsting for Christ' as well as for theological students, we shall always read it amiss.

Notes

1 The most complete life is E. Doumergue, *Jean Calvin. Les hommes et les choses de son temps* (7 vols, Lausanne, 1899–1927). Among others, W. Walker, *John Calvin: The Organiser of Reformed Protestantism* (New York, 1969); and T. H. L. Parker, *John Calvin: A Biography* (Lion Paperback, 1987). For the early life, A. Ganoczy, *The Young Calvin* (Edinburgh, 1988).

2 On the biblical works, see T. H. L. Parker, *Calvin's Old Testament Commentaries* and *Calvin's New Testament Commentaries* (both Edinburgh, 1993).

3 On the sermons, see T. H. L. Parker, *Calvin's Preaching* (Edinburgh, 1992).

4 See A. N. S. Lane, 'Calvin's sources of St Bernard', *Archive for Reformation History* (1976), pp. 253–83. Also A. N. S. Lane, 'Calvin's use of the fathers and the medievals', *Calvin Theological Journal* (1981), pp. 149–200.

5 G. H. Williams, *The Radical Reformation* (London, 1962); W. Balke, *Calvin and the Anabaptist Radicals* (Grand Rapids, 1981).

6 P. O. Kristeller, *Studies in Renaissance Thought and Letters* (Rome, 1956), p. 24.

7 This caution is not always evident in W. J. Bouwsma, *John Calvin: A Sixteenth-Century Portrait* (New York and Oxford, 1988). Professor Bouwsma's programme is based on Kant's claim (by implication) to know Plato better than Plato knew himself (p. 5). On this basis an author can mean anything that we want him to mean. Calvin said A; he thought he meant A; our more sophisticated eyes can spot the tell-tale signs which show that, influenced unawares by X and Y, he really meant B. This seems to me the end of meaningful commerce with the past (or with the present either; supply 'Professor Bouwsma' for 'Calvin' in the previous sentence, and then where are we?).

8 See Parker, *Calvin's New Testament Commentaries*, pp. 60–108.

9 C. Phillips, *Robert Bridges: A Biography* (Oxford, 1992), p. 304.

10 *The Institution of Christian religion* (London, 1634), sig. *2^r.
   A word on the translations may be useful. The first, by Norton (London, 1561), is still the best as being closest to the original. The second, by John Allen (3 vols, London, 1813), has not a few misinterpretations. But it is better written than the third, by Henry Beveridge (3 vols, Edinburgh, 1845–46), which is a more accurate translation but somewhat stodgy. The Library of Christian Classics edition, by F. L. Battles (3 vols, London, 1960), has too many blatant errors of translation but its editorial notes, taken largely from *Opera Selecta*, are useful. The best Latin edition is in vols III–V of *Calvini Opera Selecta*, ed. P. Barth and W. Niesel (Munich, 1957–62).

Part One

The knowledge of God the Creator

1 THE WHOLE SUM OF WISDOM[1]

The opening sentence of the *Institutio* sounds as a call to the Church and to the Renaissance world in a way reminiscent of Wisdom crying 'at the gates, at the entry of the city, at the coming in at the doors' (Prov 8:1–3): 'Well-nigh the whole sum of our wisdom (of that which must be considered true and solid wisdom) consists in two parts, the knowledge of God and of ourselves' (I.i.1, III.31[6–8]). The first edition had spoken more narrowly of 'sacred doctrine'. 'Our wisdom', introduced in 1539, made the sentence comprehensive.

Wisdom lies in knowing God and knowing oneself. This seminal statement is the theme of the whole of the *Institutio*. It will be found to be true in regard to God the Redeemer no less than to the Creator. The two parts are interconnected; Calvin does not conceive of two knowledges but of one twofold and interdependent knowledge. The existence of either is not possible without the other.

But does man know God in knowing himself? Or does he know himself in knowing God? Man cannot contemplate himself without thinking of God, since it is in God that he lives and by God that he is moved (Acts 17:28). He cannot claim to be the source of the good things he discerns within himself. He is led by them to God as if he were following a stream to its spring. Conversely, in discerning his own weakness and poverty he will be led to the infinite riches of God. In particular, self-perception will reveal that, as heir to

13

Adam's Fall, he is 'an unhappy ruin' (i.1, 31^{18-19}), 'empty and famished' (i.1, 31^{20}), ' a huge mass of disgrace' (i.1, 31^{24}); that he is ignorant, empty, poverty-stricken, weak, depraved, corrupted (i.1, 31^{26-28}). Until he is aware of this, his true character, he cannot have any knowledge of God. When once he knows himself, however, he realizes that 'the true light of wisdom, solid virtue, perfect affluence of all good things, and purity of righteousness' (i.1, $31^{28}-32^1$) are found only in God. He will therefore turn to him to bestow what he himself lacks.

This, however, is no easy or natural step, for to man's unhappy state it is added that he is unaware of it, self-deceived into thinking himself righteous, sound, wise and holy, almost a demigod. He assesses himself by the standards set up by his own self-love.

Thus, whether from his endowments or from his wretchedness, man's self-knowledge bears with it the knowledge of God.

Or we could start from the knowledge of God. The knowledge of God's goodness, righteousness, wisdom and power leads directly on the one hand to the realization that all the goodness, righteousness, wisdom and virtue in man are the kindly gifts of God and on the other to the awareness of his own wretchedness and poverty.

The question as to order is left undecided. Since he must start from the one or the other, Calvin chooses the path from knowledge of God to knowledge of man, as more convenient for teaching.

How is it that Calvin already knows these things about God and man? He is not claiming some inherent wisdom that enables him to know God either by intuition or by deduction from data, for, as we shall see, both these roads to knowledge are blocked. The answer is shown by his appeals to Scripture; he knows because he has been taught by Holy Scripture. From its very beginning the *Institutio* teaches and practises a theology of revelation.

What, however, do we mean by 'knowledge'? The term must be explained before he can take up the argument. This Calvin does in chapter iii: 'What it is to know God and the End at which Knowledge of him aims'. He does not investigate psychologically or metaphysically the nature of the act of cognition. His interest lies in that which is known and the effect of this knowledge upon the knower. Hence speculation and curiosity are excluded. Man is granted such a knowledge as concerns himself and leads to the honouring of God, such a knowledge as bears within itself *pietas et religio*, 'godliness and religion'.

Here for the first time Calvin brings out into the open the limitation he accepts in Book I: *The Knowledge of God the Creator*.

'I believe in God the Father almighty, Maker of heaven and earth.' He is not, he says, talking yet about the knowledge of God the Redeemer in Christ, but only of 'that first and simple knowledge to which the true order of nature would lead us if Adam had remained sound' (ii.1, 34[13–14]). It will become clear that the distinction is not between God the Creator and God the Redeemer, but between man's knowledge of the Creator and his knowledge of the Redeemer. Man cannot think, nor the theologian write, two things simultaneously. Each knowledge has to be considered on its own. Yet there is no removing of Christ from the scene. The Son no less than the Father and the Spirit is comprehended in 'God the Creator'. The Wisdom of God, the pre-incarnate Christ, is present and active in this first Book.

Merely to be aware that God exists and should be worshipped is not genuine knowledge. (We note in passing that Calvin advances no proofs for the existence of God. The next chapter will show why this is unnecessary.) In one long sentence he gives the content of the knowledge of the Creator:

I take [what I have said] like this: Not only did [God] once create this world and go on upholding it by his infinite power, governing it by his wisdom, preserving it by his goodness, and ruling in particular the human race by his righteousness and judgement, bearing it up by his mercy, and guarding it by his protection, but also, since there will nowhere be found one drop either of wisdom and light, or of righteousness or power or uprightness or of sincere truth, which does not flow from him and of which he himself is not the cause, we learn to expect and seek all things from him and to ascribe to him with thanksgiving what we have received. (ii.1, 34[30]–35[2])

The knowledge of God begets *pietas* and *religio*.

These two terms will be kept in Latin, because their English counterparts, 'piety' and 'religion', have lost their original brightness. By *pietas* Calvin meant 'a revering and loving of God, brought about by the knowledge of his blessings' (ii.1, 35[3–5]). *Religio* is 'faith combined with an earnest fear of God, a fear that both contains a voluntary reverence and also carries with it the true service and worship prescribed in the Law' (ii.2, 37[8–10]).

This passage is couched in biblical, even New Testament, terms: faith, trust, the godly mind, Lord and Father, the just Judge, the judgement seat, 'loving and revering God as Father' (37[5]), 'loathing to offend him' (37[7]), 'the worship prescribed in the Law' (37[10]). We are a pole apart from natural theology or the cool, detached acknowledgement that there is or was a creator of the universe.

All this being so, the object of the knowledge of God cannot be a god who has no dealings with man or his world and of whom the question has therefore to be asked, 'What is God?' – *quid sit Deus?* Here the hidden opponents are the neo-Epicureans. If God is as he has been described, the God who cares actively for his creation and who therefore deserves man's *pietas* and *religio*, such a question as 'What is God?' betrays a complete lack of knowledge of God, apart from being unlawful curiosity about God's essence and majesty. The proper question is already correlative with the answer it will receive: 'What is God like? – *qualis sit Deus?* – and what is appropriate to know about his nature?' (ii.2, 35[12–14]). The twofold question has been, and continues to be, answered by what is said in chapter ii about God.

The way is now open for Calvin to proceed to the main argument of chapters iii–ix. There are two conceivable ways of arriving at the knowledge of the Creator. Each, however, proves ineffectual. A third way leads to the knowledge of the Creator with its attendant *pietas* and *religio*. In doing so, however, it also validates the two hitherto ineffectual ways.

2 STILL-BORN KNOWLEDGE OF GOD

As we proceed to the first ineffectual way it will be illuminating to look on chapters iii and iv as two *loci* drawn from Romans 1:18–32 and in particular from 1:19–23. It is this passage above all which lies behind and directs Calvin's thinking here. His exposition in the commentary is too long to examine in detail and can be read separately. A fairly literal translation of the text in Calvin's rendering will be: 'For out of heaven is God's wrath revealed on all impiety and unrighteousness of men, who suppress God's truth unrighteously. For what is known about God is manifest to them; for God manifested [it] to them. Indeed, his invisible things, understood by his works from the creation of the world, are perceived, even his eternal power and divinity – in order that they might be inexcusable.'

Commenting on this passage Calvin makes most of the points that come in *Institutio* I.i–v. The notable exception is that he does not turn to Cicero's *De natura deorum* ('On the nature of the gods') to interpret it, as Martin Bucer in his commentary had done. Even in the *locus* (i.e., *Inst.* I.iii) Cicero is kept very much in the background, and appears only twice, in support of subsidiary points. Calvin's argument hinges on the clause *eis to einai autous anapologētous*, 'in order that they may be without defence'.

Chapter iii begins by laying down an axiom drawn from universal experience: 'We advance as incontrovertible that there is in the human mind a certain awareness of a Divinity' (iii.1, 37^{16-18}). Any excuse of ignorance that might be made is undercut. God himself has set within all men a perception of his existence, which he incessantly keeps fresh in their minds by instilling 'new drops' of it. His purpose in so doing is not simply that all without exception might know that he exists and is their Creator, but that they may be condemned out of their own mouths for not building on this awareness by worshipping him and consecrating their lives to his will. The only evidence needed is the universality of religion. This demonstrates that 'the sense of a Divinity is engraven in the hearts of all' (iii.1, 38^{10-11}).

Here, then, is an apparent possibility of knowledge: all men know God in that he has set the knowledge of himself within their consciousness and keeps it perpetually alive. But chapter iv at once negates the possibility: 'Just as experience declares that God sows the seed of *religio* within all, so also we shall find scarcely one in a hundred who nourishes what has been conceived in his heart, and none at all in whom it comes to maturity, far less that any fruit should appear in due time' (iv.1, 40^{31}–41^2). (It is this sustained image of 'seed', 'conceived', 'comes to maturity' and 'fruit' that is the justification for the title of this section, 'The Still-born Knowledge of God'.)

Some slide into superstition, others deliberately abandon any notion of a deity, but all fall away from the knowledge set within them. Hence no true *pietas* exists in the world, for, as we have seen, *pietas* and *religio* stem from the knowledge of God. But surely superstition is a forgivable fault, the faltering steps of simple minds that know no better? Not so; superstition is a blindness, and is nearly always involved with futility (*vanitas*), pride and stubbornness. It does not apprehend God as he offers himself, but substitutes in his place a humanly imagined something. Thus an abyss is opened, so broad that a step in any direction means destruction. Worship or obedience to God are impossible because their object is not God but an imagination, an empty dream.

But what of the atheists, theoretical and practical, the atheistical neo-Epicureans who allowed their deity no commerce with the world? They, no less than the superstitious, have the seed of the awareness of God sown in their consciousness at birth or conception. They try desperately to smother the *lux naturae*, the light they have by nature, in order that they may live freely, without restraint from God. Their god is therefore 'imprisoned idly in heaven' (iv.2, 42^{2-3}), deprived of his power as Judge and of his Providence. Such god as they have left is only 'a dead and empty idol' (iv.2, 42^{16-17}). In the last resort it can only be characterized as 'a brutish oblivion of God' (iv.2, 42^{23-24}).

The title of the chapter has, therefore, been filled out: 'That this Knowledge has been either smothered or corrupted, partly by Ignorance, partly by Malice'. All that man has to show for the awareness of Divinity engraven in his mind is the superstitious worship and servile, forced fear of gods of his own contriving. The seed has not brought *pietas* and *religio* to birth.

The second apparent possibility of knowing God is treated in two parts. The title of chapter v declares 'That the Knowledge of God is clearly apparent in the Workmanship of the World and in the continual Government of it'.

The universe, considered as a whole and in each of its parts, is a most skilfully and beautifully ordered structure. Its symmetries are mirrors in which the otherwise invisible God may be contemplated. We need only open our eyes and we shall behold him – not directly and in his inapprehensible essence, but indirectly by means of the marks of his glory engraven on his workmanship. These marks are so clear and prominent that they deprive even the dullest and most stupid of any excuse for ignorance.

But where does Calvin learn that it is the glory of God that is engraven on the universe, that the structure was made and is kept in being by God? Only from Holy Scripture, to which he turns immediately for proof of his argument, quoting Psalms 104:2–4, 11:4 and 19:1ff., Hebrews 11:3 and Romans 1:20. (Indeed, the argument stated in the previous paragraph could read as a loose paraphrase of Romans 1:19–23.)

After glancing at the terrestrial sciences and at astronomy he turns his attention especially to man himself, man as body and soul, 'an exceptional example of God's power, goodness, and wisdom' (v.3, 46^{34}–47^1). In man we find the universe in small; he is a microcosm, a little world in himself. The term is classical, but it is to

Scripture that Calvin appeals again – Paul's sermon at Athens (Acts 17:22–31) and Psalm 8:4ff.

That God has engraven marks of his Divinity on his created workmanship has needed only three paragraphs to state. The fourth begins with the death-knell of this apparent source of knowledge also: 'But here is uncovered the foul ingratitude ["neither gave him thanks" (Rom 1:21)] of men' (v.4, 47[27]). They cannot help being aware that the many benefits they enjoy are signposts, directing their minds to the Divinity; but they suppress this awareness ['who hold down the truth in unrighteousness' (Rom 1:21)] and substitute something called 'nature' as their creator in place of God.

Calvin now confronts the neo-Aristotelian doctrine which tied 'the faculties of the soul to the body so that the soul cannot exist separately' (v.5, 48[26–27]). Such a view opens the way to discussing man as a purely natural entity, 'nature' being substituted for God. In opposition, Calvin insisted that the soul has its own distinct existence. It engages in metaphysical pursuits, in physics and astronomy, in technology and the arts; it has the faculty of thinking and imagining things long past and can in sleep even foresee the future. Far from its immortality being known only by revelation (as the Mantuan philosopher Pietro Pomponazzi (1462–1525) had taught), the soul bears indelibly on itself the signs of its immortality, signs which point to its Creator, Lawgiver and Judge. To look for creation from nature itself or from some 'secret inspiration' is to deprive God of his true being and thus to be left with a something which cannot worthily be feared, believed in and worshipped.

Calvin is not urging his readers to ignore nature, but to allow it to direct them to the God of nature: 'Whenever any of us considers his own *nature*, let him remember that there is one God who governs all *natures* in such a way that he wishes us to look back to him and would have our faith directed to himself and would be worshipped and invoked by us' (v.6, 50[29]–51[1]). The possibility of knowing God through created nature is open to all men, but with the condition 'if they will follow the sketched outlines which in earth and sky give a shadowy representation of his living image' (v.6, 51[19–21]).

Nature may also be transcended. The Creator of nature shows his power not only in nature, but also apart from the ordinary course of nature. Such is the way in which he governs humanity and its society by his Providence, blessing the godly and showing severity to the wicked. From this it is easy to deduce his mercy and kindness and also his just anger. But at once Calvin shows that it is Scripture that prompts the deduction, for he turns to the seven instances of the Lord's goodness in Psalm 107. Yet 'scarcely one in a hundred' will 'praise the Lord for his goodness and the wonders that he doeth toward the children of men', so sunk in error, so blind are they.

The evidences of God's Divinity and power have been adduced rather sketchily; Calvin will consider them more fully later. Now, however, he is working towards the climax of the chapter. He first reminds us that the knowledge of God of which he is treating is not 'empty intellectual speculation' but 'what will be substantial and fruitful if we receive it aright and it strikes root in our hearts' (v.9, 53^{12-14}). God is to be known, not by attempts 'at penetration into searching out his essence' (v.9, 53^{20}), which would be audacious curiosity, but 'by contemplating him in his works' (v.9, 53^{22}), where he comes close to us and in a sense communicates himself to us.

So we come to the *peripateia*, the reversal of the situation. First the substance of chapter v is summarized:

> Therefore we must confess that in each of God's works, but especially in their universality, his attributes (*virtutes*) are really and pictorially portrayed. Thus he sweetly invites the whole race of mankind to the recognition of himself and to its consequence of true and complete happiness. (v.10, 54^{19-24})

'But', begins the next paragraph, 'we are so senseless that we are always dull in the face of such clear witnesses and they disappear without profit' (v.11, 55^{3-6}). We contemplate the creation without a thought of its Creator. We interpret events as chance and not as Providence. Or if we imagine that there is some god behind it all, we construct him according to our own dreams. And this is the source of all the errors about God in the world. The human mind is like a labyrinth in which each thinker will wander down the passage he thinks most likely to bring him to his desired end. The confusion and speculation are universal; even the great thinkers, the philosophers who try to penetrate into the heavens, show an incredible variety of opinions – Stoics, Egyptian mystics, Epicureans, all fighting one another and putting forward their notions of a god that is nothing. The conclusion is that 'men who are taught only *naturally* have no certain, substantial, clear-cut knowledge, but are attached to confused principles and worship an unknown god' (v.12, 57^{22-24}).

The verdict is: 'thus, what is left is that God shall bear witness about himself from heaven' (v.13, 58^{34}); and the next paragraph opens with the uncompromising words 'Therefore in vain . . .'. The creation does indeed proclaim the Creator's glory, yet 'these shining lamps' cannot of themselves lead us to the knowledge of him. They can 'kindle some sparks', but these are smothered before they can give a bright light. Here Hebrews 11:3 is definitive; the worlds are patterns (*simulachra*) of things invisible, but it is by faith that we understand that they were ordered by the Word of God. In other words, 'the invisible Divinity is indeed represented by such sights, but we have not the eyes to perceive them unless they [our eyes] are enlightened by an inward revelation of God through faith' (v.14, 59[7-8]).

Yet, although we are unable to reach the true knowledge of God in this way, we have no excuse for ignorance of God, since the fault and blame for the ignorance lies in ourselves. We are *anapologētoi*.

3 THE FRUITFUL TEACHING OF SCRIPTURE[2]

'Therefore' begins the next chapter as if it were the clinching of a syllogism. The awareness of a deity imposed upon every mind and the marks of Divinity engraven on all the parts of the universe are unable, through man's ingratitude, to lead to the knowledge of the true God. They serve only to make man inexcusable. The third and effectual possibility is to be taught by God himself: 'For anyone to arrive at God the Creator he needs Scripture as his Guide and Teacher', as the title of chapter vi puts it.

When God had chosen the Jews as his own flock he enclosed them within the pale of the Law to keep them from straying out into the religions and morals of their neighbours. In the same way he has given the Holy Scriptures, which he 'not only uses as teachers to educate the Church but in which he himself also opens his own most holy mouth' (vi.1, 60[31]–61[1]). Using another metaphor, Scripture is like a pair of spectacles. If you have bad eyesight you cannot read even the most beautiful print. Put on your spectacles and it all becomes clear. The universe is God's most beautiful and clear handwriting. Mankind lacks the eyes to decipher it. Learn from Scripture the relationship between God and the universe, and the signs of his Divinity will everywhere become clear.

Scripture is not merely 'another help', but also a 'better help', for in it God reveals himself as the Creator; that is, he does not merely teach his people to look to a God, but shows himself as the God to whom they are to look. Nor is Scripture an afterthought, brought in as a last resort. The order God observed from the beginning was to use his Word as well as the other helps. This was how Adam, Noah, Abraham and the rest obtained that 'familiar knowledge' which distinguished them from the heathen.

It is clear that Calvin is not suggesting that Scripture contains information which has only to be read and understood for the relationship of Creator and creature to become plain. It has also to be believed. The knowledge that God is Creator is faith-know-ledge. Hence we notice that in this chapter Calvin is addressing 'the Church', 'the elect', that is, those who already believe in God and his Word.

However the patriarchs arrived at what God made known to them, whether it was by means of visions and oracles or by human agency, they were convinced that it came from God. At last the 'oracles' (i.e., unwritten traditions) were committed to writing. Thus came the Law and afterwards the Prophets. The main object of the Law was to teach how God and man are reconciled. But besides this teaching on faith and repentance and this setting forth of Christ the Mediator, Scripture also ascribes to God the Creator sure marks and signs, thus distinguishing him from all false gods.

Man is like a spectator in 'this most splendid theatre of the world'. He must use his eyes to good effect to contemplate the works of God; but above all, his ears must be attentive to the Word. The reason why men, 'born in darkness', grow more and more hardened and stupid is because they will not listen peaceably to God when he speaks. If we are to be illuminated with true *religio* 'we must make a beginning with the heavenly teaching, for only he who becomes a disciple of Scripture can receive the merest taste of right and sound doctrine' (vi.2, 63^{6-9}). The beginning and principle of true understanding is reverently to embrace what God witnesses about himself in Holy Scripture: 'We must, I say, come to the Word where in reality and to the life God is delineated for us from his works. Then those works will be assessed, not by the perversity of our own judgement but by the rule of eternal truth' (vi.3, 63^{25-28}). Once turn aside from Scripture and we lose our way and all hope of reaching the goal of knowledge is gone. Put it another way. The knowledge of God is like an inextricable labyrinth. Whichever avenue a man takes he comes to a dead end. He can reach the centre, the glory of God, only by following step by step 'the thread of the Word' (vi.3, 64^2). Stumbling along this way, clinging to the thread, we arrive more surely than by running at top speed without it.

Although the door is now open to listening to what the Scriptures declare about God the Creator, there are still one or two necessary positions to secure.

The first is the authority of Scripture. So far this has been assumed. Now it must be considered more carefully, so that readers may accept its teaching without doubts and hesitations. Even so, the discussion will only be sufficiently thorough to fit the main argument; it will not be exhaustive (and indeed there is no comprehensive treatment of the doctrine of Scripture as the Word of God in the *Institutio*). Moreover, there can be no question of attempting to prove from external data that the Scriptures are the Word of God. All that can be done is to state the fact and explain reasons for the statement. Believers do not need the proof; they already have a sufficiently strong conviction: '[the Scriptures] obtain full authority among believers only because they are convinced that they came from heaven – as if they were there listening to the living sounds of God's own voice' (vii.1, 65^{14-16}).

The authority of Scripture does not rest on any basis external to itself. It does not rest even on the decisions of the Church. Luther had early moved step by step to the position which was from then on common to all the Reformers, that Scripture had supreme and unique authority over the Church. Johannes Cochlaeus opposed this with his *De authoritate ecclesiae et scripturae*, 'On the authority of the Church and Scripture' (1524). The title represents the contents by putting Church before Scripture and thus in a sense above Scripture. Calvin is here rebutting both Cochlaeus and also Johannes Eck, whose *Enchiridion* (1532) had the same purpose.

To make the authority of Scripture depend on the authority of the Church was, for Calvin, to make it depend on human decisions. He has already in earlier chapters rejected the validity of man's judgement in regard to the knowledge of God. Hence men cannot assure us that the teaching of Scripture is from God; only God can do this. Nor can they assure us that the message has come down to us whole and entire. But what of the determination of the 'canon' that this document is to be regarded as part of Scripture whereas that is to be excluded? Does not, therefore, the Church determine what is Scripture? And what is this but saying that the authority of Scripture depends on the authority of the Church?

Calvin's reply is to expound Ephesians 2:20: '[you are] built upon the foundation of the Apostles and Prophets'. The Church is built on the teaching, not the persons, of the Apostles and Prophets. But the apostolic teaching is contained only in Scripture. Therefore, far from being the production of the Church, the substance of Scripture antedates the Church and is itself the Church's foundation. Nor will it do to assert that the Church determined the teaching by decreeing what books were to be included in the canon. Rather, what the Church was doing was assenting to the authority which the various books of the Bible exercised over it. Should anyone still wish to step outside this circle and ask *how* we are convinced that the teaching is from God unless we trust the word of the Church, he should in return be asked how he has learnt to distinguish light from darkness, white from black, sweet from bitter. It is self-proving.

Chapter vii has already said that it is God himself who speaks in Scripture. This central point is now elaborated. Scripture itself everywhere bases its authority on the fact that God is speaking: 'The Prophets and Apostles assert neither their own acuteness nor anything that wins trust for speakers; nor do they take their stand on reasoning. They bring forward the holy Name of God, by which the whole world is forced into obedience' (vii.4, 69$^{1-4}$). We are, therefore, outside the realm of probability (and hence doubt and instability), even outside the realm of human reasoning. Here there is only the conviction that God himself is addressing us, a conviction born of 'the secret testimony of the Spirit' (vii.4, 69^{11}).

To try to prove the authority of Scripture by rational arguments would be working back to front. First must come the firm conviction, and only afterwards the very powerful arguments which he says he will soon bring forward. Such arguments will not produce the assurance that *pietas* needs, for they are of no weight compared with the testimony of the Spirit, that is, by the Holy Spirit giving an inward conviction that what is read or heard is the voice of God. 'Therefore the same Spirit that spoke by the mouth of the Prophets must penetrate into our hearts to convince us that they faithfully delivered what God had committed to them' (vii.4, 70$^{5-8}$).

Calvin's expression for this is that Scripture is *autopiston*, self-authenticating. Negatively, it neither needs nor can have proof from outside itself. Positively, it really and actively proves itself. To call this a circular argument would be correct but misleading. Better to regard it under the image of an electrical circuit which must not be short-circuited from outside itself. Once it is posited that God can be known only in that he reveals himself, then it must follow that the form in which he reveals himself can be known to be the form of revelation only by revelation.

The consequence is that in Scripture we are confronted by mystery. None, so the chapter concludes, with allusion to Matthew

13:11, can understand the mysteries of God save those to whom it is given. Only those 'who are inwardly taught by the Holy Spirit' (vii.5, 70^{16-17}), 'who are illuminated by his power' (vii.5, 70^{22-23}), will be completely convinced that Scripture is from God, that it has come 'from the very mouth of God' (vii.5, 70^{26-27}). They feel 'that there an undoubted power of the Divinity is active and breathes' (vii.5, 71^{1-2}), so that 'we are drawn and set on fire to obey him wittingly and willingly' (vii.5, 71^{2-4}).

It would be easy to misunderstand Calvin's next steps unless careful attention is paid to his words. Having taken his stand unambiguously on the self-authentication of Scripture, he now seems to short-circuit the electrical circuit with arguments from without. Thus Allen's translation renders the title of chapter viii 'Rational Proofs to Establish the Belief of the Scripture'. He had been preceded by the fearful section 6 of the Hundred Aphorisms: 'God the Creator is also [!] known in the Holy Scriptures. We must consider of what nature they are, namely true and proceeded from God's Spirit; which is proved by the testimony of the Holy Spirit, by the efficacy and antiquity of the Scriptures, by the certainty of the prophecies' and by the other arguments in chapter viii. In fact, the title of the chapter is: 'That there are, so far as human Reason can manage, sufficient Proofs firm enough to support the Credibility of Scripture'. The first sentence supplies the necessary 'stage-direction': 'Except there be this certainty [i.e., the certainty by the testimony of the Spirit] which is higher and stronger than any human judgement, it will be futile to fortify the authority of Scripture by arguments or to support it by the consensus of the Church, or to strengthen it with other aids. Unless this foundation is laid it will always remain uncertain' (viii.1, $71^{39}-72^3$). It is, therefore, clear that chapter viii is not to be read as a set of proofs of the authority of Scripture as the Word of God in addition to the testimony of the Spirit. Without the testimony of the Spirit they are useless; for the believer already convinced that God speaks to him in the Bible they are valuable supports.

In chapter viii we leave Cochlaeus and Eck. There can be little doubt that the editors of *Opera Selecta* were correct in directing us to the Parisian free-thinkers (III.70 n.1). Scepticism and apparently intelligent contempt on the part of educated people often raise doubts in the minds of even firm believers as to whether the Bible is to be trusted. To say to such Christians that they already believe the Bible to be the Word of God is right and necessary. But this is not precisely their problem. Rather, it is that their faith has somehow been misplaced or must somehow or other be modified to fit informed contemporary opinion. ('Somehow' well fits the uncertainty.) They do not see that scepticism does not and cannot be relevant where God is concerned, that there can be no breaking into this circuit. Therefore, pastoral care for those 'hungering and thirsting after Christ', doctrinal care for the theological students, demanded a reasoned *apologia* to demonstrate the baselessness of the free-thinkers' attack on the Bible.

The six or seven arguments that Calvin deploys (all taken from the Apologists of the second century or current among the Church fathers) are intended to show that, granted the premise that Scripture is from the Holy Spirit, there is nothing in the Bible inconsistent with the Spirit. Thus, the more we study Scripture the more we wonder at how well-ordered is 'the dispensation of the Divine Wisdom' (viii.1, 72^9), at how the teaching is everywhere 'heavenly and in no way earthly' (viii.1, 72^{9-10}). The very fact that in the main the literary style of the Old Testament has 'a contemptible baseness in language' (viii.1, 72^{16-17}) is by God's Providence, for this crude style has more power than all that the art of the rhetorician can give, because under it are delivered the sublime mysteries of the heavenly kingdom.

No need for us to run through the other 'proofs' – the antiquity of Scripture, Old Testament miracles, the preservation of the Old Testament, the writing of the sublime truths of the New Testament by 'unlearned and ignorant men', the indestructibility of Scripture in the face of continual attack, and so on. All are treated in the same way; the same conclusion is reached at the end of each, that we are forced to see that our faith in Scripture is not misplaced. But at the last Calvin comes back to the original statement that 'in themselves they lack the strength to provide faith [in Scripture] until the heavenly Father takes reverence for it out of the realm of controversy by revealing his Divinity there. Scripture will suffice for the saving knowledge of God only where there is a grounded assurance by the inward convincing of the Holy Spirit' (viii.13, 81^{20-25}).

The free-thinkers, however, were not the only enemy to be faced and overcome if the principle of *Scriptura sola* was to be maintained. A wing of the Anabaptists was equally destructive. Hence chapter ix: 'That those Fanatics who disregard Scripture and flit away to "revelation" overturn all principles of *pietas*'.

A new movement, Calvin says, has arisen which wants a direct, unmediated relationship with God. Its adherents think that because they have the Holy Spirit dwelling within them, guiding them, enlightening them, they do not need Scripture. They are adult, spiritual Christians, despising the childish followers of the dead letter.

But what 'Spirit' have they in mind? If it is the Holy Spirit, their claim is exposed in all its absurdity. For were not the Apostles and the other early believers illumined by this Spirit? And did they despise as a dead letter what they themselves wrote? Or again, is their 'Spirit' the same that Christ promised to send to his disciples? But that Spirit would, according to Christ, give them the understanding of his teaching, which is handed down in Scripture. The office of the Holy Spirit is to seal and impress in our minds the teaching of Scripture; and if this is so, anyone who wishes to be genuinely 'spiritual' must read and listen to Holy Scripture. The Spirit, the author of Scripture, has 'impressed his image' on Scripture.

It is true that Scripture can be a dead letter, a letter that kills (2 Cor 3:6); but it is dead and death-dealing precisely when it is separated from the grace of Christ and is a mere sound in the ears, leaving the heart untouched. 'But if it is efficaciously imprinted in hearts by the Spirit, if it manifests Christ, then it is "the Word of life", "converting the soul", "giving wisdom to children" etc.' (ix.3, 84^{5-8}). (Calvin is alluding to Psalm 19, already cited in v.1 and vi.4, thus making it a thread running through his argument.) When our minds have 'the substantial *religio* of the Word, the Spirit so shines that he makes us see God's face there' (ix.3, 84^{17-18}). In spiritual matters self-deception (or being deceived by Satan) is all too easy. In the Word there will be no deception, for there we recognize the Spirit in his image. The only illumination claimed by the arrogant *enthousiastai*, those who boast they are literally filled with the Divinity, is what they dreamed when they were asleep. God's children 'know of no other Spirit than he that lived and spoke in the Apostles and by whose proclamations they are unremittingly called to the hearing of the Word' (ix.3, 85^{1-3}).

4 GOD THE CREATOR

Before the doctrine itself is considered, the compatibility of the sources has to be established: 'it is now important to see whether God displays himself to us in Scripture as just the same that we earlier saw sketched out in his works [of creation]' (x.1, 85^{9-12}).

27

What is shown in the creation is a sketch, a delineation, an outline. In Scripture God displays himself 'more familiarly and clearly' (x.1, 85^{8-9}). Nevertheless, the sketch and the manifestation are completely consonant.

Besides the general picture of God in Scripture as a good and kind Father who is yet strict in his condemnation of evil, there are places 'where his genuine "face" is manifested for us to see it *eikonikōs* [as in an image or portrait]' (x.2, 86^{7-8}). The passage he chooses to expound is Exodus 34:6: 'Jehovah, Jehovah, the merciful and kind God, patient, of much compassion, and true, who keeps mercy for thousands, who takes away iniquity and sins, with whom the innocent will not be innocent, who renders the iniquity of the fathers to the children and grandchildren.'

By the noble name 'Jehovah' we are taught God's eternity and *autousian* (self-existence). The passage also manifests his attributes (*virtutes*) or qualities. By these Scripture describes God not in regard to his inner life but as he reveals himself towards us. For the knowledge of God is 'a living awareness' rather than 'an empty and aëry speculation' (x.2, 86^{18-19}). The *virtutes* are precisely those that chapter viii declared to shine forth in the creation – mercy, goodness, compassion, righteousness, judgement and truth. The name 'Elohim' comprises strength and power. Hence our own experience from beholding the creation shows us that God is no different there from what he declares himself to be in his Word.

Nor is the aim of the knowledge given in Scripture any different. It is first that we may fear God, then that we may trust him. And from this we learn to worship and serve him 'in perfect innocence of life and sincere obedience, and then to depend entirely on his goodness' (x.2, 87^{17-19}).

It is in order to direct us to the true God that Scripture 'excludes and rejects' all others. Thus the title of chapter x: 'Scripture, to correct all superstition, opposes the true God exclusively to all the Gods of the Nations'. The demonstrating that God's self-revelation in Scripture is no different from the delineation of himself in the creation was only the first step. The second, taken here, is to establish that the unity of God is also both taught by Scripture and accepted universally, if only in theory. Even those with a plurality of gods used the singular form 'god' when they spoke, showing 'from a natural awareness' that the concept of the unity of God is engraven on all hearts. But all without exception are either turned aside by their own emptiness or fall into false opinions. The result is that 'whatever they feel naturally about the one and only God is of use only that they may be inexcusable' (x.3, 88^{1-2}). Even the philosophers, the very wise men, do not escape the condemnation of corrupting the truth of God.

The third step follows the course of the Ten Commandments (this passage formed part of the exposition of the Second Commandment in earlier editions: 'Thou shalt not make to thyself any graven image nor the likeness of anything that is in the heaven above or in the earth beneath or in the waters under the earth . . .'. The previous step may be taken as expounding the First Commandment: 'Thou shalt have no other gods but me'). It may also be regarded as a *locus* on Romans 1:22: 'Professing themselves to be wise, they became fools, and changed the glory of the incorruptible God for the likeness of an image of corruptible man, and of birds, and four-footed beasts, and creeping things.' The terms in this verse provide the framework of Calvin's argument here. The title of chapter xi runs: 'That it is wicked to ascribe a visible Form to God, and that all those who set up Idols for themselves defect from the true God'.

Holy Scripture addresses itself to popular errors rather than to the subtleties of philosophers. It therefore does not contrast the true God to false concepts of God, but to actual manufactured idols. Its opposition is, nevertheless, comprehensive, including mental images as well as material idols. The Commandment must be taken in its bald straightforward sense; God must not be represented by any visible image: 'God does not compare images with one another, as if one were more, another less, fitting. Without exception he rejects all images, pictures, and other signs by which the superstitious imagine they will have him near them' (xi.1, 89^{3-6}). Those who seek 'visible forms of him' are in fact departing from him, for God is not known by sight but by the hearing of his voice or Word (Deut 4:15: 'you heard a voice; you did not see a body').

Certainly, when God revealed himself by way of signs, they were so true and certain that he was in a sense seen 'face to face'. But the signs all served at the same time as concealment, so that, in revealing, they preserved the incomprehensibility of his being. In Deuteronomy 4:11 God's presence was hidden by clouds, smoke and flames, which were yet 'symbols of the heavenly glory'. When the dove descended on Jesus at his Baptism it was 'a momentary symbol' of the Spirit who himself was invisible. The cherubim above the mercy seat were certainly images, but the purpose of them was to conceal the mercy seat with their wings. The signs and symbols in the Bible must not be taken, therefore, as precedents for making representations of the Deity.

The emphasis now moves away from the idolatry of the heathen to images sanctioned by the Church. Even the Eastern Church is at fault, for the Second Commandment prohibits not only sculptures but also likenesses in the form of pictures and icons. They are often excused as books for the illiterate; but this cannot be sustained in the face of the scriptural rejection of images as not genuinely representing God. What the illiterate learn from images and icons is, therefore, not the true likeness of God. The true image of God and Christ is the preaching of the Gospel and the holy Sacraments. In the Gospel, as Paul wrote to the Galatians, 'Jesus Christ crucified was plainly pictured before your eyes' (Gal 3:1). Images are not true representations of God, but projections of their maker's own being: 'the flesh never rests until it has got a likeness to itself which will bring it empty comfort as an image of God' (xi.8, 97^{21-23}).

There is, however, a legitimate use of the plastic arts. 'Because sculpture and painting are gifts of God, I desire a pure and legitimate use of both' (xi.12, 100^{27-28}). God should not be represented in a visible form, because he has forbidden it and it cannot be done without deforming his glory. What, then, may be subjects for the artist? 'It remains that only those things may be painted and sculpted which can be seen by the eye' (xi.12, 101^{5-7}). By 'seen by the eye' he means historical or fictional subjects or, without reference to a story, 'images and forms of bodies'. The former are useful as teaching aids; as for the latter, 'I do not see what they can bring apart from delight' (xi.12, 101^{9-11}) – the delight is clearly accepted as legitimate.

Calvin recognizes that much in chapter xi is negative. He therefore shows positively in chapter xii why idolatry is to be rejected: 'God is to be distinguished from Idols in order that he alone may be truly worshipped'. Again he reminds us of the foundations he has laid in the first two chapters. The knowledge of God is not a cold speculation, but bears with itself the venerating of God. It is the difference between *religio* (which, with *pietas*, is the fruit of the knowledge of God) and *superstitio* which, 'not content with the limits and the way prescribed, heaps up a superfluous mass of empty things' (xii.1, 105^{25-27}).

Worship must conform to the nature of God. Just as God himself has his own existence and is not the fiction of human thinking, so also worship, or the honouring of God, is not something to be devised according to human religious, aesthetic, or moral predilections, but must correspond to the being and nature of God. In this lies the difference between *religio*, *pietas* and *superstitio*.

What then is the God like (*qualis sit Deus*) who must be so worshipped and served? 'That God's unique Essence or "Being", which contains three Persons within itself, is taught in the Scriptures from the very Creation.' Holy Scripture throughout discloses God's being as the being of Trinity, and that from its first chapter in the account of the creation.

The specific mark by which God is to be distinguished from the gods of men is that, while he reveals himself as one and singular, he at the same time reveals his existence in three 'Persons'. In this the true God is distinguished from all false gods. Since such a doctrine is at first sight a denial of the unity and uniqueness of God, a division into three deities, a short and simple definition must be found to correct this impression.

Calvin uses Hebrews 1:3 for his definition. A close rendering of his own translation will be: 'Who, since he is the splendour of his glory and the character of his substance . . . '. It is the second term that concerns us now – *charaktēr hypostaseōs autou*, *character substantiae eius*. In his commentary on Hebrews Calvin explains the reasons for his rendering: *charaktēr* he defines as 'a living form': 'God is truly and actually known in Christ. For his image is not merely some obscure outline but the express likeness which bears his form, as a coin does the matrix of the die from which it is struck. Yet the Apostle is saying more than this – that the Father's substance is in a sense insculpted in Christ. The word *hypostaseōs*, which I have rendered "substance", denotes to my mind not the being or essence of the Father but his "Person" . . . It is truly and appropriately said that whatever the Father has as his own is expressed in Christ' (CO 55, p. 12). This, he says, is how the orthodox fathers used *hypostasis*, so that there is a threefold *hypostasis* in God but a single *ousia* or essence.

Calvin's treatment of the doctrine of the Trinity grew through the three recensions of the *Institutio*, not in importance but to fit the conditions at each stage. The catechetical *Institutio* turned to Ephesians 4:5–6 ('one Lord, one Faith, one Baptism, one God') and used Baptism as the initial argument. There is but one Baptism and one God. But Christ commanded Baptism to be administered 'in the name of the Father and of the Son and of the Holy Spirit' (Matt 28:19), 'And what is this but to testify clearly that the Father, the Son, and the Holy Spirit are one God? For if we are baptized into their name, we are baptized into their Faith. Therefore, if they are worshipped by one Faith, then they are one God' (OS I.71[20–23]).

This argument continues to make an appearance in the 1539ff. *Institutio*, and its position as prefacing the exposition of the Creed is also kept. In the 1559 edition, with the exposition of the Creed being dropped, the doctrine of the Trinity could no longer form the preface, and is now given a chapter to itself, but still in the wider context of the knowledge of God the Creator and in the narrower context of the true God being distinguished from idols.

Words and concepts from early Christology like *hypostasis* or *prosōpon* sound little like the teaching of Scripture to which Calvin is committed, and there were those who were hypercritical about the use of non-Biblical words, who thought that theologians should 'keep not only their thoughts but also their words within the bounds of Scripture and not scatter the seed of alien terms, which would only be a seedbed of disagreements and quarrels' (xiii.3, 111[16–18]). It depends, Calvin says, what they mean by 'alien'. If it is just the words themselves, it is a ridiculous principle, for 'any interpretation which was not patched together out of the fabric of Scripture' (xiii.3, 111[23]–112[1]) would be condemned. But if 'alien' means something devised for the sake of curiosity, that is more contentious than edifying, and leads away from the simplicity of Scripture, he entirely agrees: 'a sure rule of both thinking and speaking must be sought out of the Scriptures, and all the thoughts of our minds and the words of our mouths should be directed strictly to that rule. But what prevents us, when there are things in Scripture that perplex and hinder our understandings, from explaining those things with plainer words, so long as they preserve the truth of Scripture religiously and faithfully and are used sparingly, moderately, and seasonably?' (xiii.3, 112[9–15]).

Nevertheless, Calvin could wish the technical language buried, so long as there was this common Faith, 'that the Father and the Son and the Spirit are one God; yet that the Son is not the Father, nor the Spirit the Son, but that they are distinguished by a certain "property"' (xiii.5, 113[31]–114[2]).

It is only now in paragraph 6 that, 'arguments about words left aside', Calvin comes to his statement proper: 'I call "person" a subsistence in the being of God, which, related to the others, is yet distinguished by an incommunicable property. By the word "subsistence" we intend something other than essence [or "being"] to be understood' (xiii.6, 116[12–15]). In his French translation Calvin renders *substantia* as *résidence*, a no less elusive term. But from what follows it is clear that he really has moved on from words and derivations to definitions and scriptural explanations. The passage just quoted ends with proof from John 1:1, to the effect that there would be no point in the words 'and the Word was with God' if the Word were simply God, with no property of his own. The name 'God' used indefinitely refers to the Son and the Spirit as well as to the Father. There is, therefore, a relationship or relatedness in the being of God. But each subsistence has its own incommunicable property, 'so that whatever is ascribed to the Father as a distinguishing mark can neither belong to nor be ascribed to the Son' (xiii.6, 116$^{29-30}$).

There is no need to follow the detailed demonstration from Scripture of the Deity, first of the Son, then of the Spirit. We merely note that the demonstration is from Scripture and that it fits contemporary conditions rather than those of earlier centuries. In particular Calvin's target is Servetus who, in his books *De Trinitatis Erroribus* ('On the Errors of the Trinity'; 1531) and *Dialogorum de Trinitate libri duo* ('Two Books of Dialogues on the Trinity'; 1532), had taught a sixteenth-century version of Sabellianism.

What follows is a consideration of the relationships within the Deity. Now the starting point is the Incarnation. This does not mean that Calvin has crossed the dividing line between Creator and Redeemer, but, as Christ's coming was a clearer revelation of God than was given in the Old Testament, so it was a clearer revelation of God's threefold being. At this point Calvin makes use of his old material from 1536 on Baptism being into one God but in the name of the three Persons: 'from which it is plain that in the being of God there reside three Persons, in whom the one God is known' (xiii.16, 130$^{8-9}$).

Explanations of this doctrine are dangerous, not dangerous so much rationally as religiously. When all has been said this 'is a great mystery. We should walk with the utmost awe and soberness' (xiii.17, 131$^{1-2}$). So he commends a sentence from Gregory Nazianzen's oration *On Holy Baptism*, which, unusually, he quotes entirely in Greek: 'I am not able to think the One without being surrounded by the brightness of the Three; nor can I distinguish the Three without at once being brought back to the One' (xiii.17, 131$^{3-7}$).

The Church fathers sometimes used analogies to cast light on this mystery. Calvin is no doubt thinking particularly of Augustine, with his analogies drawn from a man's single being but with three

33

different qualities within that being. Calvin himself is more than doubtful about both the value and the wisdom of such attempts. In their place he draws from Scripture general qualities ascribed to each Person and presents them in relatedness: 'There is attributed to the Father the origin of activity and the fount and wellspring of everything; to the Son wisdom, resolution, and the administration in the performance of things; to the Spirit is ascribed the power and effectiveness of the activity' (xiii.18, 132$^{9-11}$). This implies a certain ordering; but it is not a temporal order of before and after, for the three Persons are coeternal. In this order, 'first is considered the Father, then, from him, the Son, afterwards, from both, the Spirit. For the spontaneous inclination of the mind of anyone is first to consider God, then, emerging from him, Wisdom, and finally the Power by which the decrees of his purpose are executed' (xiii.18, 132$^{16-20}$).

The scriptural distinction in no way infringes the unity of Persons and oneness of God. We can prove from it that the Son is one God with the Father because they have one and the same Spirit, and that the Spirit is not different from the Father and the Son because he is the Spirit of the Father and the Son. If either Person is considered separately, he is thought of in his being as God. But in reference to the Persons, there is the relationship and distinction of Father–Son, Father–Spirit, Son–Spirit.

The rest of the chapter (paragraphs 21–29) consists of refutations of heresies – not so much the ancient heresies, except in so far as they were echoed or elaborated in his own day, as attacks on the doctrine which had recently been made and which had caused trouble in Reformed communities, and particularly in Geneva. In 1558, at the very time that the new *Institutio* was being written, the Italian Church in Geneva was thrown into theological turmoil by the Trinitarian speculations of some of its members. To restore peace, they were required to subscribe to a confession of faith. All but one ultimately signed: seven, however, very unwillingly; of these, one, Valentine Gentile, was imprisoned for persisting in his errors. He, with another Italian, Blandrata, and the Spaniard Servetus, is the object of Calvin's polemic in these paragraphs.

5 GOD'S CREATURES

(i) The world

The title of chapter xiv shows that Calvin is still keeping firmly to his argument: 'It is in the very Creation of the World that Scripture by sure Marks distinguishes the true God from fictitious Gods'. We have now moved on to the activity of the Trinity as Creator. At the same time it is still a question of recognizing the true God from his activity; not directly from the contemplation of the created universe, but from the revelation in Scripture of the universe as God's creation. Calvin therefore turns first to the accounts of the creation in Genesis 1 – 2. But after only two paragraphs he leaves that place to consider the inhabitants of the heaven which God created, and then the sphere of wickedness and the devils. Only then does he return, for three paragraphs, to Genesis. We also note that he clearly wishes chapters xiv and xv to be taken together by starting paragraph 3 with the words 'But before I begin to discuss more fully the nature of man . . . ' and chapter xv with 'And now we must speak of the creation of man'.

God's purpose in revealing the creation story was that the Church should believe it and seek only the God whom it declares to be the author of all things. Calvin first deals with the question of time. He is, of course, operating within the chronological framework of a creation occurring within the fifth millennium before Christ; but the date is not the ruling factor. Rather he is considering time as finitude, so that believers may not only be led back by the thread of time to 'the first origin of the human race and of all things' (xiv.1, 152^{16-17}), but by arriving at the beginning of time itself, and seeing there the Creator, may recognize his eternity. Questions of date like 'Why did not God create the universe sooner?' are silly and irrelevant.

Moses' account of the creation is, therefore, like a mirror 'in which is reflected the living image of God who is invisible and whose wisdom, power, and righteousness are incomprehensible' (xiv.1, 153^{10-13}). God's self-revelation as Creator is by means of that which he created, but this only when he himself testifies to it and explains it in the simple terms of an oral tradition of his original revelation to the first humans. If the creation story is a mirror, it is also, in regard to the one who sees the created things and hears the account, the pair of spectacles that we met earlier: 'For just as eyes that are dim with age or weak from some defect can make out nothing clearly without the aid of spectacles, so (such is our weakness!) unless Scripture directs us in seeking God, we forthwith fail and faint helplessly away' (xiv.1, 153^{13-16}). With the spectacles which are Holy Scripture, looking at the mirror which is Genesis 1 – 2, we shall not lose ourselves in infinity of time or unlimited space. It is impudence to complain against God that the emptiness is a hundred times greater than the universe. The obsession with infinity of time and space is a cupidity, a coveting to go outside the world. 'Therefore let us willingly remain enclosed within these bounds in which God's will has circumscribed us, and let us, so to say, contract our minds so that they do not drift off in libertarian wandering' (xiv.1, 153[35–37]).

Here we have no close exposition of Genesis 1 – 2. No doubt we are meant to read the relevant parts of Calvin's commentary on Genesis, which had appeared five years before this *Institutio*. At any rate, in this chapter there are only brief and general mentions of parts of the creation, which, as a whole, demonstrates 'God's fatherly love towards the human race' (xiv.2, 154[12]) and in which 'he undertakes as a provident and careful Father the care of his family' (xiv.2, 154[18–19]) – a statement of the utmost importance for the rest of the *Institutio*, not least for the teaching on the Sacraments.

(ii) The Angels

The Apostles' Creed obliquely, the Niceno-Constantinopolitan Creed directly, speak of a part of the creation that is invisible. 'We must insert something about the Angels' (xiv.3, 154[28]). Calvin has to leave Genesis 1 – 2, which has no reference to Angels, and move off to later places in Genesis where they appear as God's ministers and hence, by inference, as a part of his creation. The silence of the creation story need not prevent us from assembling and ordering the general teaching of Scripture on Angels. It is certainly a subject that ought to be treated, if only because of the wild theories that have been imagined. Yet the rule holds good here, too; the rule demanded by *pietas*, that we must not wander away from the simplicity of faith: 'in this, as in all religious teaching, a single rule of modesty and sobriety is to be observed. In matters obscure we should neither speak nor think nor even seek to know anything but what is delivered to us in God's Word. A second is that when we read Scripture we should keep within bounds and in our seeking and meditating dwell on what makes for edifying and not indulge our curiosity or a concern for useless things' (xiv.4, 156[18–24]).

Such a rule would not fit pseudo-Dionysius, the author of *The Celestial Hierarchy* (c. 500). Anyone would think, Calvin says, that he had come straight out of heaven with a first-hand account of what he had seen. But the most of it is mere idle chatter. 'The task of a theologian is not to please the ears with talk but to strengthen consciences by teaching what is true, certain, and useful' (xiv.4, 157[11-13]). Calvin's way will be to consider 'what God wishes us to know about his Angels from the simple teaching of Scripture' (xiv.4, 157[19-20]).

He begins with the generalization that in Scripture Angels are 'heavenly spirits whose ministry and obedience God uses to execute everything that he decrees. The name [*angelos* = messenger] is given them because God employs them as go-betweens (*internuntios*) in manifesting himself to men' (xiv.5, 157[21-25]). He uses them to effect everything that he determines.

The Angels are also called a Host or an Army, surrounding their Prince like attendants to magnify his greatness and majesty, and like soldiers ever watchful for a sign from their Leader and so ready to carry out his command that they are engaged in the work by the time the command is given. Again, because God exercises and administers his dominion over the world through them, they are called Principalities, Powers and Dominions. They are even said to be Thrones, 'because in a certain sense the glory of God resides in them' (xiv.5, 158[1-2]) – but this is not the better interpretation of Colossians 1:16, Calvin admits, and, therefore, should not be pressed. Yet it is right to pay honour to the Angels as 'the instruments by whom God especially reveals the presence of his Divinity' (xiv.5, 158[7-9]). They are more than once called 'gods', because in their ministry 'they partially represent to us the Divinity as in a mirror' (xiv.5, 158[10-11]).

But the main emphasis in Scripture is that 'they are the dispensers and administrators of the Divine beneficence towards us' (xiv.6, 158[24-25]); they guard our safety, defend us, direct our paths and watch over us. Whether each individual has his own 'guardian Angel' is doubtful from the scriptural evidence, and is not really a comforting doctrine, for every one of us is surrounded and escorted by troops of such helpers.

Calvin turns next to the scriptural teaching on the devils. Here, too, the subject is dealt with chiefly in regard to believers. The aim of Scripture is to forewarn believers, so that they may arm themselves and rely only on God, wrestling against the Devil all through their lives. There is not just one enemy, but a whole host, 'great armies', ruled by a prince. Christ is the Head of the Church; the impious, and *impietas* itself, have a prince, the Devil.

But are we not dealing with the creation and its Creator? Is, then, a part of the creation evil? Certainly, the Devil was created by God; but he was created good; the malice of his nature springs from his defection and fall. About this Scripture speaks only sparingly and gives us no information at all about its why and when and how. Therefore 'let us be content to hold merely this on the nature of the devils: that at their first creation they were Angels of God, but by degenerating they ruined themselves and became the instruments of ruin for others' (xiv.16, 166³⁶⁻³⁸).

To speak of war and discord between Satan and God demands qualification. It is not a question of there being two equal but opposing forces, for God is always the All-mighty Lord. Hence it must be said that Satan 'is not able to do anything unless God wills and assents' (xiv.17, 167⁸⁻⁹), as is clear from many places in Scripture, e.g., Job 1:6; 1 Kings 22:20ff.; Psalm 78:49; 2 Thessalonians 2:9, 11. But this does not exculpate Satan or show that he is obedient to God, for by nature he is bent on enmity against God and strives to oppose him in everything. Yet he is bound by God and can do only what God permits. Satan in Calvin's sermons on Job bears a strong resemblance to the Caliban whom Shakespeare created a half-century later in *The Tempest*.

In regard to believers God is in control of the devils as they assail them: 'they harass them with fighting, attack them in ambushes, trouble them with attacks, press hard on them in battles, often wear them down, trouble them, frighten them, sometimes wound them, but never conquer or overwhelm them' (xiv.18, 167³⁹–168³). This is a lifelong warfare. Some battles will be lost. But Jesus Christ has won the victory; in him it is completed; for his members the victory appears only 'in part' until at death they are freed from the weakness of the flesh. On the contrary side the Devil has been given power over the ungodly; they have degenerated from their true nature into the image of Satan.

(iii)   The human race³

Calvin returns to the visible creation, 'this most beautiful theatre', there for men to contemplate as the workmanship of God; not only to look at what is without, but also at themselves as God's creatures. Yet to treat chapter xv as Calvin's 'doctrine of man' without qualification would be to take the wrong turning by interpreting him as, at this point, if not transformed into a thoroughgoing Renaissance humanist, at least so influenced by contemporary humanism as to admit a foreign element into his scriptural theology. It is easy to pick out quotations which seem to support such a view. Man 'is the most noble and notable specimen among all the works of God' (xv.1, 173$^{28-29}$); 'in the outward man is reflected the glory of God' (xv.3, 176^{38}); 'the many wonderful gifts that the human mind possesses and which cry aloud that something Divine is engraven on it are so many testimonies of its immortal essence' (xv.2, 175$^{21-24}$).

All such praises of man are common among the humanists. We find Pico della Mirandola (1463–94) imagining the Creator address-ing Adam with the words:

> Neither a fixed abode nor a form that is thine alone nor any function peculiar to thyself have we given thee, Adam, to the end that according to thy longing and according to thy judgment thou mayest have and possess what abode, what form, and what functions thou thyself shalt desire. The nature of all other beings is limited and constrained within the bounds of laws prescribed by Us. Thou, constrained by no limits, in accordance with thine own free will, in whose hand We have placed thee, shalt ordain for thyself the limits of thy nature . . . We have made thee neither of heaven nor of earth, neither mortal nor immortal, so that with freedom of choice and with honor, as though the maker and molder of thyself, thou mayest fashion thyself in whatever shape thou shalt prefer. Thou shalt have the power to degenerate into the lower forms of life, which are brutish. Thou shalt have the power, out of thy soul's judgment, to be reborn into the higher forms, which are divine.[4]

Or, at any rate, next to divine. For a little later he writes, now in his own person:

> Let us disdain earthly things, despise heavenly things, and, finally, esteeming less whatever is of the world, hasten to that court which is beyond the world and nearest to the Godhead. There, as the sacred mysteries relate, Seraphim, Cherubim, and Thrones hold the first places; let us, incapable of yielding to them, and intolerant of a lower place, emulate their dignity and their glory. If we have willed it we shall be second to them in nothing.[5]

What Pico had said in his solemn oration in 1486 was to be repeated in lively fashion by the Spanish humanist Luis Vives in his *Fabula de homine*.[6] It is too long to summarize here, but is well worth reading for amusement.

We must see whether Calvin conforms to this humanist view of man in chapter xv: 'In what sort Man was created. Where also are discussed the Faculties of the Soul, the Image of God, and the primal Integrity of Nature'. His opening sentence shows that the emphasis is going to be on man as God's creation, not on man as a being in his own right: 'We must now talk of man's creation, not only because he is the most noble and remarkable example among all God's works of his justice and wisdom and goodness, but because, as we said at the first [i.e., I.i.1], God cannot be known clearly and genuinely by us unless there is also added the mutual knowledge of ourselves' (xv.1, 173$^{27-31}$).

Even more distinctive is what follows. Renaissance humanists held at best only an attenuated doctrine of the Fall and sin. Man may fall below the high place allotted to him; if he does, it is a disaster but not fatal. Calvin, however, at once posits a twofold self-knowledge, 'as we were made in our first origin' and 'what our state began to be after the Fall of Adam' (xv.1, 173^{33}). By doing this he has tied this chapter in with the early chapters of Book II on sin. For the present, however, man is to be considered in his unfallen state. Why, when that state has been lost? Because, if we were to proceed straight to man as he now is, the evil that is natural to him (Calvin is careful not to say 'his evil nature') might be blamed on the author of his nature, God, thus providing an escape from inexcusability. But 'the ruin of the human race is to be treated in such a way that every escape route is blocked and God's righteousness vindicated from any accusation' (xv.1, 174$^{14-17}$).

The first thing to be said of man's creation is less than flattering. He was formed of clay. Hence 'nothing is more absurd than for them to glory in their own excellence who not only inhabit a mud hovel but who are themselves partly earth and ashes' (xv.1, 174$^{20-21}$). What Adam had to glory in was that God intended him to be the dwelling-place of an immortal spirit. For man is composed of both body and soul, which is sometimes called 'spirit', although there is a distinction between them. The soul is 'an immortal but created essence' (xv.2, 174$^{27-28}$), as is proved both by the conscience, which distinguishes between good and evil, and by the fact that man is able to know God (for a non-immortal energy could not attain to the fountain of immortality).

Again, man's many excellent endowments declare that 'something Divine' is engraven on his mind, thus testifying to an immortal essence. His intelligence is more than sensory; it has the ability to search out nature, investigate history, arrange in order, infer a probable future from the past. It can go so far as to conceive of an invisible God and Angels. It can grasp what is right, just and honourable. Calvin is here rejecting tacitly the view of the soul that we noticed earlier and which is found in the book by Pietro Pomponazzi, *On the Immortality of the Soul* (1516).[7] Starting out from what he found a worrying difference between Aquinas and Aristotle on the nature of the soul, Pomponazzi expounded all the views with which he was acquainted and decided for the inseparability of soul and body. Examining the various arguments for the immortality of the soul, he concluded that this cannot be proved. Nevertheless, he accepted it on the authority of the Church. Against this, Calvin insists on the separability of body and soul, and on the possibility of the immortality being proved.

The fact that man was created in God's image is one proof. The proper seat of the image of God is the soul. The image expresses Adam's integrity, in that he had a right understanding, affections or emotions adjusted to reason, all the senses in harmony, together with the awareness that all these were gifts from God. By the image he was raised above the rest of the visible creation.

We need to examine more closely the faculties in which man excels if we are to have a full definition of the image of God. This can best be learned from considering the restoration of the image through Christ: 'the aim of regeneration is that Christ shall re-form us to the image of God' (xv.4, 179^{18-19}). For Paul (Col 3:10) this renewal means knowledge, righteousness and holiness. Thus we infer that originally the image was apparent in 'the light of the mind, uprightness of heart, and soundness in all the parts' (xv.4, 179^{26-27}). Similarly 2 Corinthians 3:18: ' "we with unveiled face beholding the glory of God are transformed into the same image". But Christ is the most perfect image of God and it is to that image that we begin to be formed in such a way that we bear the image of God in true *pietas*, righteousness, purity, and understanding' (xv.4, 180^{4-5}).

Thus we arrive at the full definition: 'God's image is the perfect excellence of human nature which was reflected in Adam before his Fall . . . in some part it is now manifest in the elect in so far as they are regenerate by the Spirit, but it will reach its full splendour in heaven' (xv.4, 180^{19-24}).

This is quite different from the Manichaean doctrine, recently revived by Servetus. Because the soul is the breath of life breathed into man by God, it means that the soul is a transmission of the substance or essence of God. If so, replies Calvin, then God's essence is weak, subject to change, sinful, ignorant. The soul came into being, not by transfusion, but by being created out of nothing. Nor are believers regenerate according to God's image from an 'inflowing of essence, but by the grace and power of the Holy Spirit, who most certainly does not make us consubstantial with God' (xv.5, 182^{11-12}).

An understanding of the nature of the soul is not to be sought from the philosophers. Only Plato saw that the image of God is in the soul and is an immortal essence. Others placed it either partly or entirely in the body. Against them must be set the Scriptures, which teach that the soul is an incorporeal essence. Although it is not spatially limited, it dwells within the body as a house where it 'not only animates all the parts of the body and makes the organs fit and employable for their activities, but also holds the pre-eminence in ruling man's life – not only in regard to the earthly life but also in that it incites man to the worshipping of God' (xv.6, 182^{26-30}). It might be objected that there is little evidence of this in practice. But it has already been taken as an axiom that a certain awareness of God is imprinted on men's minds and that man was created to meditate and practise the heavenly life. Hence, 'the more one studies to approach to God, the more he proves that he is endowed with reason' (xv.6, 183^{7-8}).

Although he speaks appreciatively of Plato's doctrine of the soul, he finds it too complicated and presents a simplified version. The soul consists of two parts, the understanding, or intellect, and the will. The task of the understanding is to distinguish between the objects set before it and either accept or reject them. It is, there-fore, 'the leader and governor of the soul' (xv.7, 185^{11}). The task of the will is to choose and follow what the understanding calls good and reject that of which it disapproves. All the powers of the soul are comprehended under these two parts. The light of reason is a guide, *to hēgemonikon*, a Stoic term. To this God has added the will, with the power of choice, directing the appetites and harmon-izing their movements.

In his integrity man possessed freedom of will. By choosing aright he could have arrived at eternal life: 'Adam could have stood had he wished, seeing that he fell only by his own will' (xv.8, 185^{5-6}). But, because his will was flexible and because he was not given the constancy to persevere, he fell so easily. The philosophers confused man before and man after the Fall, and so were able to ascribe free will to fallen man: 'They looked for a building in a ruin, for well-fitted connections in a dispersion' (xv.8, 186^{12-13}). But why did not God give man constancy? We do not know. Our wisdom lies in sobriety and submission to his revealed truth.

6 PROVIDENCE

The name 'Creator' has not been fully understood when God is called only 'the Maker'. This is why chapter xvi begins with the word *Porro*, 'Furthermore'. What has still to be said appears in the title: 'By his Power God cherishes and guards the World which he made and by his Providence rules its individual Parts'.

That God is a 'momentary Creator', performing one single task, can be the opinion only of unbelievers. Faith sees that 'unless we go further, to his Providence, we have not yet really grasped what it means that God is the Creator' (xvi.1, 187^{19-21}). Neither the universe as a whole nor its individual parts are activated by some 'universal movement', the philosophers' 'secret inspiration of God', but by God's individual Providence upholding, cherishing and caring for everything that he made, down to the least sparrow (Matt 10:29). What is lacking in the unbeliever's opinion is above all the scriptural insistence on God's special and Fatherly care for the individual.

From the outset it becomes clear that Calvin's concept of Providence is intended to be drawn from Scripture. He is not interested in metaphysical problems of the relationship between Divine cause and earthly effect. He will have none of the Epicurean or quasi-Epicurean separating of God from his creatures. Instead there is the comforting doctrine that we and all things are in the hands of our almighty heavenly Father.

Calvin first opposes Providence to fate or chance. The common opinion has always been that events are fortuitous; 'but whoever learns from the mouth of Christ that all the hairs of his head are numbered will seek further for causes and conclude that all events whatsoever are governed by the secret determination of God' (xvi.2, 189^{8-11}). Even inanimate objects are included. Certainly, they have their individual properties, according to which they exist and are effectual; but they cannot exert their power apart from the hand of God being present to direct them. The sun is the most powerful of all inanimate things, warming men and beasts, causing seeds to germinate and grow into fruitful plants. But that the sun is not the principal or necessary cause but merely an instrument used by God is proved from the fact that, according to Genesis 1, God created not only light but also herbage before the sun. Again, the miracles recorded in Joshua 10:13 and 2 Kings 20:11 show that the sun's rising and setting are not governed by 'a blind instinct of nature', but by God himself, 'to renew the memory of his Fatherly grace toward us' (xvi.2, 190$^{7-8}$).

What has been said is an affirmation that God is almighty. Calvin's understanding of this omnipotence has now to be explained, for the Reformers considered it had been perverted by the Schoolmen with their distinction between *potentia absoluta* and *potentia ordinata*. The former, 'absolute power', meant the power which God could exercise if he wished and to which there could be no limits (apart, of course, from the logically absurd). *Potentia ordinata*, 'ordered, or disposed, power', is that which God has actually displayed. Calvin does not here use the term *potentia absoluta*, but refers to it obliquely as the concept held by 'the Sophists'. Such a power was only potential and, therefore, 'empty, idle, and almost sleepy' (xvi.3, 190$^{15-16}$). God's omnipotence, on the contrary, is 'awake, effective, and continuously active' (xvi.3, 190^{16}). It is not that he could act if he wished to but in fact does not act, but that 'governing heaven and earth by his Providence, he so directs all things that nothing happens but by his determination' (xvi.3, 190$^{23-24}$). The 'philosophical' interpretation of Psalm 115:3, 'all that he willed he did', is very weak. What afflicted believers receive comfort from is the belief that they suffer nothing but by the ordination of God and that they are in his hands.

A right view of God's omnipotence is doubly fruitful. First, in that God has abundant ability to do good, for he possesses all things and all creatures are destined to his service. Secondly, that we can safely rest in his protection, because anything harmful is under his control; even Satan is forcibly bridled by his power. It is, therefore, superstitious to fear anything created, for example the stars as having power over events or careers. All things are 'so ruled by the secret determination of God that nothing happens but by his knowing and willing decree' (xvi.3, 192$^{11-12}$).

The right view of Providence is that God does not look down from heaven as an idle spectator but that he, so to say, holds the helm. Thus it is not simply a question of God's 'eyes' (pro-vidence, over-seeing) but also of his 'hands'.

Calvin now moves away from the Epicurean view to consider the idea of 'universal Providence'. He will not condemn outright this whole position, but asks that its exponents will on their side concede that God rules the world 'not only in that he preserves and guards the order of nature which he himself has laid down but in that he has a particular care of every one of his works' (xvi.4, 194^{10-13}). He agrees that 'every species of things is moved by a secret instinct of nature as if it were obeying an eternal command of God and is proceeding spontaneously because God had once appointed it' (xvi.4, 194^{13-15}).

Take, first, the succession of days and seasons. They say that God predetermines a firm law. But then, what of droughts, cold wet summers, warm winters? How on that basis can these be the work of God? In any case, there is no place in all this for God's Fatherly kindness or for his judgements. Nor is it consonant with Scripture, where all natural events are directly ordered by God ('not a drop of rain falls but by the definite command of God' – xvi.5, 195^{25-26}). Even things that we call accidents are seen in Scripture as ordained by God. Nothing could be more chancy than the casting of lots, but Proverbs 16:33 says that the result is disposed by the Lord.

Particular events are in their own way testimonies to God's individual Providence. Examples in Scripture are the wind that brought the quails to the Israelites (Num 11:31) and the wind that stirred up the tempest in Jonah 1:4. Those who do not believe that 'God holds the helm of the world' (xvi.7, 197^{19-20}) say that such events are unusual. 'But I gather from them that no wind ever rises or increases but by the special order of God' (xvi.7, 197^{21-22}). Similarly with human infertility. And even bread is the staff of life only by 'the secret benediction of God'.

Some think that this is simply crypto-Stoicism, a religious variety of Fate. Not so. The Stoics constructed a necessity within nature which arose from an involved interweaving of circumstances (cf. one of Thomas Hardy's favourite phrases, 'by a curious concatenation of circumstances . . . '). 'Our' doctrine, on the contrary, is that 'God is the governor and controller of all things; by his wisdom he determined from all eternity what should come to pass, and now by his power he effects what he had decreed' (xvi.8, 198^{26}–199^1). This is clearly an extremely definite and exclusive doctrine, and Calvin at once imagines the incredulity of the reader: ' "What!" you will say, "does nothing happen fortuitously or contingently?" ' (xvi.8, 199^{4-5}). For reply he quotes Basil of Caesarea: 'Fortune and chance are heathen words; their mere sense ought not to enter into believers' minds' (xvi.8, 199^{6-7}). If in human affairs success is God's blessing, adversity his curse, no place is left for fortune or chance.

Nevertheless, he concedes that there is a difficulty to be resolved and makes a distinction between the actuality and the appearance. The actuality is God's Providence; the appearance is what we perceive. 'Although all things are ordered in the purpose of God by a sure administration, yet to us they are fortuitous' (xvi.9, 200$^{6-7}$). Not fortuitous in the sense that the world is ruled by 'Fortune', but because the reason, purpose and necessity of events are hidden in God's counsel and cannot be grasped by human thought. He imagines as example a merchant travelling with companions through a wood, imprudently wandering off by himself, getting lost, and being attacked and killed by a gang of robbers. How are these events to be interpreted? From the point of view of Providence it must be said that God had not merely foreseen his death, but had determined and fixed it. From our point of view, however, the whole affair has been fortuitous, a chapter of accidents.

The relationship between Providence and contingency comes down to the different senses of the word 'necessity'. Here Calvin accepts and uses, although characteristically simplifying it, the very complex mediaeval distinction between different sorts of necessity. His argument starts from the statement that 'whatever changes are seen in the world proceed from the secret activity of the hand of God' (xvi.9, 201$^{19-20}$). But then: 'What God determines is necessary to happen in such a way that nevertheless it is not a necessity positively nor from its own nature' (xvi.9, 201$^{20-22}$). As scriptural example he takes Psalm 34:20, quoted in John 19:33, 36, 'He keepeth all his bones: not one of them is broken'. As Christ had a human body, his bones were breakable. But yet it was impossible that any of them should be broken. 'So we see that the distinctions were not unreasonable that the Schoolmen made between "necessity according to which" and absolute necessity, and again between consequent necessity and the necessity of consequence. God subjected to breakableness his Son's bones which he had exempted from being broken. Thus he restricted to the necessity of his will what could naturally happen' (xvi.9, 201$^{25-30}$).

On the practical value of the doctrine to the believer Scripture teaches three main points. First, Providence is to be referred to the future as well as to the past. Secondly, that God acts sometimes through means, sometimes without means, sometimes contrary to means. And thirdly, the end of the doctrine is that God shows his care for all humanity but especially for the Church. It must also be added that God's purposes are to be revered when we do not understand them. What appears confused and fortuitous to us should be regarded as part of God's good plan. In a violent storm on earth little can be seen because of the darkness; ears are deafened and heads bewildered by the thunder; everything seems to us a wild confusion. Yet above the clouds 'quiet and serenity remain in the heavens' (xvii.1, 203$^{5-6}$).

To consider Providence in such a way will teach us humility and sobriety. We are not able to comprehend why God performs any particular action. His will in Providence is hidden from us, his judgements are incomprehensible, a great deep or abyss. There should be no attempt to discover the reason for this or that event, far less a cocksure attitude of always knowing God's purpose. His Providence is secret; his will is secret. We can only revere in awe what we do not understand.

Calvin was attacked in his own day for positing two wills in God, the one revealed in the Law and the Gospel, the other kept hidden from men. And certainly there are statements in paragraph 2 which seem to give grounds for this criticism. In the next chapter, however, he faces the problem squarely: 'They object that if nothing happens except as God wills, then there are two contrary wills in him, so that he determines in his hidden will what he openly forbids in his Law. This is easily resolved' (xviii.3, 224$^{3-5}$). Calvin points to the many scriptural passages from which he draws his doctrine, culminating in the statement in Acts 4:28 that Herod and Pilate 'conspired to do what the hand and counsel of God determined'. It is not that God is double-willed, but that we are simply unable to understand how he can both wish and not wish the same thing. We think that because God's wisdom is what Ephesians 3:10 calls *polupoikilos*, 'many-sided', there must be changeableness or inconsistency in God. This is only the foolishness of our human minds, which cannot grasp the mind of our Creator.

The central question is how God can be free from guilt if he uses wicked men, and even Satan, to achieve his purposes. It was to take the sting out of this problem that theologians had made the distinction between God's action and permission. But God himself tells us in Scripture not that he permits actions, but that he himself acts. 'Therefore whatever men, or even Satan, may practise, God holds the helm and converts all their efforts into the executing of his judgements' (xviii.1, 220$^{17-19}$).

Against this it is objected that it makes God the author of men's wickedness. Calvin replies that the objection rests on the confusion of two distinct concepts, will and commandment. His elucidation consists entirely of exposition of some scriptural stories, principally the account of the election of Jeroboam as king (1 Kings 11:26 – 12:20) and the treachery of Judas, recorded in all four Gospels. On this last he quotes Augustine with approval: 'The Father delivered up the Son, Christ delivered up his own body, Judas delivered up the Lord. Why, in this "delivering up", is God righteous and man guilty, except because in the self-same thing that they did the reason for doing it was not the same' (xviii.4, 227[6–9]). Judas (and hence by analogy Satan and the reprobate) had no intention of obeying the declared commandment of God, but acted in opposition to it. He was rebelling against God; yet God's gracious will used Judas's crime for the redemption of mankind. God remained untainted, for he had no share in Judas's sinful motives.

We return to the Christian's attitude to Providence. How does such a doctrine affect our life? We might shift the blame for our sins from ourselves to God – all things happen by God's will, so how could I help sinning? We could let it drive us to despair and ultimately to suicide – 'this is my destined fate'. We could, on the other hand, neglect to take any precautions against dangers – God has determined the hour of my death and there is no point in seeking to evade it (General Gordon!). We could regard it as only reasonable to give up praying – if God has predetermined everything, prayer is redundant. Finally, we could lapse into complete irresponsibility and amorality.

But God has given us both foresight and the means to preserve life. It is, therefore, our duty to use the means. Prudence and sound advice are not at all inconsistent with Providence, for 'they are breathed into men by the Lord and subserve his Providence' (xvii.4, 207[24–26]).

Objection: Why should crimes be punished if they are predetermined? Answer: God has told us in his Word what he demands of us; it is this that we must follow. Further objection: But unless God willed it, the crime would not have been committed. Answer: True, but it does not excuse the criminal, whose motive has been wrong. He was not acting in order to obey God's will, but from some form of selfishness. Yet God knows how to use even evil instruments for his own good purpose without being defiled.

Believers will reckon with secondary causes. They will thank others for kindnesses; they will blame themselves for slackness or imprudence in business or in not caring for the sick as they should have done. For future events they will use shrewdness and commonsense and will take advice from others. Yet they will look to Providence as the principal cause even while acknowledging secondary causes. When they trust God as the keeper of themselves and all things, they will show gratitude for his blessings, patience in adversity and an incredible freedom from anxiety about the future. If they suffer unjustly, they will look up to God, who will bring their mind to patience so as not to dwell on wrongs but to forgive the offenders. If the adversity is only one of the commonplace troubles of life, they will accept it as from the Lord no less than the blessings they enjoy.

Minds framed thus are immeasurably happy. Otherwise, life will be misery as we worry about the many dangers we face: 'Board a ship and you are only a foot from death. Mount a horse, and your life is jeopardized by a single stumble. Walk through the streets of a city and you are as liable to as many accidents as there are tiles on the roofs' (xvii.10, 214^{21-24}). We may try to comfort ourselves by saying that it will not happen to us; but we cannot be sure and, therefore, cannot have peace of mind. The believer dares to commit himself to God, knowing that it is his heavenly Father who rules the universe and, therefore, all the events of his own life.

Notes

1 General expositions of Calvin's theology are W. Niesel, *The Theology of Calvin* (London, 1956); F. Wendel, *Calvin: The Origins and Development of His Religious Thought* (London, 1963). On the knowledge of God see E. A. Dowey, *The Knowledge of God in Calvin's Theology* (New York, 1952); T. H. L. Parker, *Calvin's Doctrine of the Knowledge of God* (Edinburgh, 1969).

2 See R. S. Wallace, *Calvin's Doctrine of the Word and Sacrament* (Edinburgh, 1953).

3 See T. F. Torrance, *Calvin's Doctrine of Man* (London, 1949).

4 Pico della Mirandola, 'Oration on the Dignity of Man', 3, in E. Cassirer, P. O. Kristeller and J. H. Randall (eds), *The Renaissance Philosophy of Man* (Chicago, 1969), pp. 224–5.

5 Ibid., p. 227.

6 Ibid., pp. 387–93.

7 Pietro Pomponazzi, 'On the Immortality of the Soul', ibid., pp. 280–381. For Pico see P. O. Kristeller, *Eight Philosophers of the Italian Renaissance* (Stanford, 1966), pp. 54ff.; and for Pomponazzi see pp. 72ff. of the same book.

Part Two

The knowledge of God the Redeemer in Christ

1 MAN THE TOTAL SINNER[1]

We come to the second Book, *On the Knowledge of God the Redeemer in Christ, which was revealed first to the Fathers under the Law and then to us in the Gospel.* We have not left Book I entirely behind us, however; it accompanies us through the present Book and, indeed, to the end. The *Institutio* unfolds, not by treating separate doctrines in succession, but by a continuous thread of argument.

We do, however, note in this Book a change of what we may call, following our original metaphor, some of the stage scenery. The references to classical authors tend to become scantier, their place being taken by the ecclesiastical writers. The first five chapters deal with one of the greater differences between the Reformers and Rome, sin as the bondage of the will. Calvin therefore takes pains to show that the original teaching of the Church (that is, Scripture and the Church fathers) had been perverted by mediaeval scholasticism and in particular by frequent misunderstandings on the part of Peter Lombard, the most influential of the earlier schoolmen. Hence large tracts of these chapters consist in effect of historical essays with special reference to Augustine and Lombard.

'Know thyself!' said the ancient Greeks. The first sentence of the *Institutio* has declared that well-nigh the whole sum of wisdom consists in the knowledge of God and of ourselves. But 'know thyself!' for Calvin did not mean 'know thy excellences', as we heard Pomponazzi saying. It means 'know thy original excellence, which was God's gift, and be grateful; know also thy present sinfulness, and repent for so corrupting God's good gift'. The typical Renaissance ethical ideal lay in learning what is virtuous and then battling to overcome the faults of character that prevent its realization. Christian self-knowledge has another aim and result, to become aware of sin and, therefore, to be despoiled of all moral confidence in order to find salvation outside oneself.

The first step in learning the true nature of sin is by examining the original Fall of man. The tree of the knowledge of good and evil was set before man as the test of his obedience and of submission to the order which God had established. Hence disobedience and, as Augustine said, pride were at the heart of the primal sin. But Calvin would probe even deeper. The root of the defection from obedience was *infidelitas*, a lack of trust in God, a lack of credit to his Word. It was from this that ambition sprang, man's ambition to be greater than was given him. And the offspring of ambition was obstinate rebellion against God.

The Fall, however, was not something that happened once to one man individually. It involved all humanity as the children of Adam. If we ask how others, at such a space of time and distance, could be implicated in the sin of another, the reply must be, not by imitation, as the Pelagians held, but by propagation. The child of sinners is a sinner. 'All we, therefore, who descend from impure seed are born infected by the contagion of sin. Before even we see the light we are defiled and polluted in the sight of God' (II.i.5, 234[11–13]). Adam was not simply the originator of mankind but the root from which the plant, humanity, sprang; and the plant is of the same species as its root. Moreover, the Fall meant a loss to humanity. God deposited with Adam the gifts he intended for all men. In losing them, Adam lost them not only for himself but for mankind. Yet the loss is not to be viewed as natural, as if the cause of the infection of sin lay in man's soul or body. It was by God's decision that the gifts should be lost for Adam's descendants as well as for himself.

Calvin defines this original sin as 'an hereditary crookedness and corruption of our nature, which is spread into all the parts of the soul' (i.8, 236[33–35]). (*Pravitas*, the word I have rendered 'crookedness', carries also the sense of deformity and perversity.) It was not merely, as was taught by, among others, Anselm, Duns Scotus and Occam, a lack of original righteousness. This does not go far enough, although it is true in itself. Our nature is not only empty of all good, but also full of all evil, an evil that cannot be idle. It is 'like a burning furnace, flaming and sparkling, or a spring endlessly gushing out water' (i.8, 238^{2-3}). Those who defined it as *concupiscentia* (e.g., Augustine, Lombard, Aquinas, Biel) are more correct, so long as the *concupiscentia* is extended to the whole man and not confined to the passions. For this is where Lombard went wrong. He took the biblical word 'flesh' as meaning physical appetite, *sensualitas*, contact with which defiles the soul. 'Flesh' in the Bible includes also the soul and thus man's reason and will. Hence there is no part of man free from sin.

God made man perfectly sound and whole. It was by his own fault that man fell from that state of perfection. To say that men are now naturally sinful seems to blame the Creator of nature for creating something imperfect. We must, therefore, distinguish between two senses of 'nature'. Man is corrupted with a natural fault, but the fault did not proceed from nature. It was alien to his original being. It may be called 'natural' only in the sense that it comes from inheritance and not by imitation.

Sin has now been understood as an active and dominating force within man. But how complete is the domination? The question is 'whether, since we are reduced to this servitude, we are despoiled of all liberty; and, if any particle [of liberty] is still active, to what extent it retains strength?' (ii.1, 241^{6-8}). The way in which this is answered will carry two distinct moral dangers. 'That Man is now despoiled of Liberty of Will and assigned to wretched Servitude' (title of ch. ii) must be so presented as to avoid, on the one hand, making men inactive ('If I am in servitude to sin there is no point in trying to be righteous') and, on the other, granting man any liberty at all, when he will at once arrogantly try to snatch at God's own honour. To steer this difficult middle course we must teach that man has no goodness of his own; but teach it in such a way that he may, nevertheless, be stirred up to aspire after goodness and his lost liberty.

At this point Calvin refers us back to I.xv.7–8, that the soul 'is sited both in the mind and the heart' (ii.2, 242^{25}). The philosophers usually think of reason as an intellectual quality, 'like a lamp illumining all the counsels [of the mind] and like a queen commanding the will . . . Sense, on the contrary, they regard as languid and half blind, ever creeping on the earth, wallowing in grossnesses, never raising itself to a clear perception' (ii.2, 242^{27-33}). For the will to obey reason is virtue; if sense is in control, man is corrupted to evil. For them the remedy is that sense must be educated, disciplined and tamed. In any case, they leave the will free to choose between reason and sense.

Here Calvin relates the history of the doctrine of free will, from the fathers and into the Middle Ages. We take up the thread when he comes to Peter Lombard. Lombard makes a distinction between three kinds of freedom in man: first from necessity, second from sin, and third from *miseria* ('the bondage of corruption' in Rom 8:21).[2] The first inheres in man naturally; the others are lost by sin. Calvin accepts the distinction, but with the reservation that Lombard confuses necessity with compulsion.

We are all agreed, says Calvin, that man has no free will to do good works without the aid of the special grace given to the elect by regeneration. But here it has to be asked whether man has no power at all, or only a little that needs help. Lombard distinguishes between 'operating grace' and 'co-operating grace'; the former by which a man effectually wills the good, the latter which follows the good will with assistance. This distinction Calvin mislikes. Although it ascribes the efficacy of any appetite for good to grace, it implies that man has a desire for good of his own nature, even if this desire is ineffectual. Nor does he like the second part any better, with its suggestion that it lies within man's own power to render the first grace vain by rejecting it or to confirm it by obedience. He sets out his position as dissenting from the 'sounder schoolmen' in some respects, but decisively from the 'later sophisters' (no doubt the Pelagians or semi-Pelagians of the fifteenth and sixteenth centuries).

Calvin sees Lombard's teaching as merely coming to this: Man possesses free will in such a way that he is not free to choose between good and evil, but does evil by his own will and not by compulsion. Quite true. But what a freedom!

As he returns to the fathers, and especially to Augustine, Calvin admits that they speak with more than one voice. But the important thing is that they all give the praise for man's good to the Holy Spirit: 'I dare affirm that, although they sometimes overmuch extolled free will, their intention was to teach man to turn away from any confidence in his own power and place his strength in God alone' (ii.9, 252[13-17]). He also allows that the term 'free will' can be used in a good sense; but its implications are so dangerous that it would be better not to use it at all.

True self-knowledge is the awareness of one's wretched state as a sinner. So long as a man's intention is to look to God to supply what he lacks there is no danger of his taking too much away from himself. It is when he begins to claim just a little more than he should that he enters into the temptation of the Fall, 'ye shall be as gods'. The cardinal rule is complete humility before God.

Calvin agrees with the general view which distinguished between the 'natural gifts' and the 'supernatural gifts' bestowed on man at his creation. At the Fall the 'natural gifts' were corrupted, the 'supernatural' taken away altogether. Thus man was banished from God's kingdom and everything that belonged to the life of blessedness was extinguished until it should be recovered by the grace of regeneration. These 'supernatural gifts' are faith, the love of God and the neighbour, and an application to righteousness and holiness. The 'natural gifts' are soundness of reason and uprightness of heart. The will was not destroyed by the Fall, 'for it is inseparable from man's nature. But it was entirely conquered by perverted desires, so that it cannot desire anything right' (ii.12, 255[21–23]). Nor is the reason invalid in sinful man; but it covers only 'inferior' things: that is, political life, government, whether of communities or households, handicrafts, the liberal sciences. In regard to the knowledge of God, the order of righteousness, the mysteries of the kingdom of heaven, it is incapable.

In the 'inferior' things Calvin cannot speak too highly of reason:

What then? shall we deny that truth shone in the law-givers of old, who set forth civil order and discipline with such great equity? Shall we say that the philosophers [i.e., scientists] were blind in their carefully investigated contemplation and skilful description of nature? Shall we say that they lacked sense who, by establishing the art of speech, taught us to speak rationally? Shall we say that they were mad who, in developing medicine, employed their industry for us? What of all mathematics? Shall we think them the craziness of madmen? No, we cannot read the writings of the ancients without enormous admiration . . . But shall we think anything praiseworthy or excellent which we do not acknowledge as coming from God? Let us be ashamed of so great ingratitude! (ii.15, 258[18–31])

In regard to morality man's reason seems at first to be valid. There is a 'natural law' imprinted in his heart in the form of conscience. But how far is this of use in regulating his behaviour? Its real purpose, in fact, is only to make him inexcusable. Calvin defines natural law as 'the awareness of conscience, of discerning sufficiently between what is righteous and what unrighteous, with the object of taking away the excuse of ignorance when men are accused by its testimony' (ii.22, 265$^{8-11}$).

But may not conscience be deceived, or man be ignorant, as Plato taught? If so, where is man's responsibility for his actions? This brings Calvin to the problem of ignorance and deception in sin and their relation to responsibility. He accepts Aristotle's distinction between *incontinentia* and *intemperantia*. The former implies a moral disturbance; when someone is thrown off balance and does something wrong, repentance may follow hard upon the fault. *Intemperantia*, however, is not checked by consciousness of sin, but persists stubbornly on the evil course it has chosen.

The next three chapters pursue and emphasize the corruption of man's will. Since, according to Scripture, the 'flesh' is sinful, and since it includes the whole man, it follows, as the title of chapter iii has it, that 'From Man's corrupt Nature proceeds Nothing but what is condemnable'.

What, however, of the 'virtuous heathen', those for whom Erasmus expected salvation? Have there really been no men or women in the whole history of the world who could justly be called good and virtuous? Calvin accepts that there are such, even if not perfectly and absolutely good. Does it not therefore follow that man is not completely corrupt? He further accepts that in such people God's grace is active. But this is not saving grace, but grace given for the sake of society. The problem has not yet been resolved, however. Either all men must be placed on the same moral level or, if a differentiation is made, a goodness in man will have been conceded. But Calvin has already said that such good gifts in the heathen come from the special grace of God. Hence they are not natural gifts. By nature even the virtuous man is corrupt. What is more, he corrupts the special grace given him so that it loses its favour with God.

The will remains in fallen man, but it is bent towards sin and cannot move to good. Deprived of liberty, it is drawn to evil of necessity. Necessity is distinguished from compulsion in that it is inward as against the outward compulsion. 'Man, as he is vitiated by the Fall, wills to sin, not unwillingly or by coercion; by an extreme propensity of the mind, not by violent compulsion; by the movement of his own desire (*libido*), not by external compulsion. He cannot not be moved and driven to evil by his depravity of nature' (iii.5, 278$^{11-15}$). This, Calvin claims, is no new doctrine but one taught by Augustine and in the monasteries for a thousand years. Lombard misunderstood it, not distinguishing between necessity and compulsion. He was also at fault in reversing Augustine's order of salvation, in which grace precedes every good work, with the will accompanying it but not going in advance. By this reversal Lombard made the will predominate over grace.

Man therefore sins necessarily; but he sins voluntarily. He is in bondage to the devil; but it is he himself that sins. Two problems arise here. The first is: 'Whether in evil actions anything is to be ascribed to God?' (iv.1, 291$^{10-11}$). The second is the relative places of the devil and man in a man's evil actions. For this Calvin borrows a simile from Augustine. Man is like a horse, with either God or the devil as rider. If God is in the saddle, the horse will be guided on the right course; if the devil, all will go wrong. Unfortunately, all the simile does is to state the same problem in pictorial terms without resolving it. The horse is the real problem in this context. It is, says Calvin, not reluctant nor restive nor coerced when the devil rides, for it has been bewitched or beguiled by the devil's deceptions and, therefore, is necessarily obedient to his leading. Therefore, 'the cause is not to be sought outside the human will, from which the root of evil springs. In the will is sited the foundation of Satan's rule – that is, sin' (iv.1, 291$^{33-36}$).

To explain whether anything is to be ascribed to God in sinful acts, Calvin leaves the metaphor of horse and rider, and takes up the classic example of Job. A band of Chaldaeans steal Job's camels. Obviously, this was a wicked deed. But the story tells us that Satan was behind it. In Job's eyes, however, it was God's work. 'How shall we ascribe the same act to God, to Satan, and to the Chaldaeans without excusing Satan as God's co-worker or saying that God is the author of evil?' (iv.2, 292$^{5-8}$). Quite easily, if we look at the motives involved and the means employed. God's motive was to exercise Job's faith and patience. Satan's motive was to make Job despair. All the Chaldaeans wanted was plunder. God's method was to permit Satan to act by handing over the Chaldaeans to his incitement to evil. Satan incited the Chaldaeans (already wicked) to steal the camels. The Chaldaeans rushed into the wickedness. Thus God's righteousness remains uncontaminated, but Satan and the Chaldaeans wicked and unrighteous.

It is high time to remind ourselves of the argument. The title promised a consideration of *The Knowledge of God the Redeemer in Christ*, but all we have been given so far is five chapters on man the sinner. The link is to be found, of course, in the word 'Redeemer'. These five chapters have been necessary to demonstrate that man is so completely a sinner that he not only is unable to redeem himself, but indeed does not wish to do so. At the beginning we were told that the knowledge of God and of ourselves are so interconnected that the one will lead to the other. So it is now. The knowledge that we are sinners brings us to consider the knowledge of the God who is our Redeemer in Christ.

2 THE CHRIST OF THE OLD AND NEW TESTAMENTS

'For lost Man Redemption is to be sought in Christ'. So runs the title of chapter vi, still laying the emphasis on man's lost state. The first paragraph reinforces this by referring us back to the still-born knowledge at the beginning of Book I: 'The genuine order was certainly that the structure of the world should be a school for learning *pietas*, from which there would be a passage to eternal life and perfect happiness. But after the Fall, wherever we turn our eyes we are met by God's curse . . . Although God wishes still to show his Fatherly grace to us in many ways, yet we cannot grasp that he is our Father from viewing the world while our conscience oppresses us inwardly and shows that our sin is a just reason for God to abandon us and not reckon or regard us as his children' (vi.1, 320[13-23]).

But, even if the two natural roads to salvation are closed, may not a third way remain open? It is a historical fact that Jesus Christ came into the world at a certain date, much later than many good and virtuous men, whether Gentile like Socrates or the Roman Camillus, or Jewish like Abraham or Moses. If it is granted that after his Death and Resurrection salvation is through him alone, what of those who lived before his Death and Resurrection? Will they not be saved on account of their outstanding virtue? Calvin will have none of this. Salvation is by God's grace alone. The Jews who lived before Christ pose a different problem, however, and this is the subject of the next five or six chapters.

The question now is whether there were in Old Testament days revelations, and therefore redemption, apart from Christ. Calvin states his position without more ado: 'God never showed himself gracious to the ancient people [the Jews], never gave them hope of grace, apart from the Mediator' (vi.2, 321[31-32]). And again: 'The blessed and happy state of the Church was always founded on the person of Christ' (vi.2, 321[35-37]) – he means the Old as well as the New Testament Church. Christ is the promised seed of Abraham. He is the truth of which David was the lively image. His kingdom is the reality which David's foreshadowed. The future fulfilment of present shadows in him was the message of all the Prophets. The Jews (that is, the godly and believing Jews) never trusted in their own Law or the special holy localities or an earthly king. Their hope 'always rested in Christ alone' (vi.3, 324[24-25]). Apart from Christ they could not have believed in God, for there is no faith in God apart from him. Therefore, 'from the beginning of the world [Christ] was set before all the elect as the one to whom they should look and in whom all their trust should repose' (vi.4, 325[39-41]).

The main thing has been said. In Christ alone God always has been, is, and always will be the Redeemer. But this requires amplification and confirmation from the Old Testament itself.

In the Old Testament we are concerned with the Law. By 'Law' Calvin means the whole system of religion handed down by God through Moses. But the Law did not come first in the history of the Jews. It was preceded by the Covenant which God made with Abraham, a covenant of promise and blessing. The Law followed, not as something new and different or contrary, but as continuation and renewal, to recall the people to the Covenant and keep them within it. But the substance of the promise to Abraham was Christ. It is, therefore, established that the Law was not in opposition to Christ.

'Law' must also be taken as including the Davidic kingdom. Hence Christ was shown to the Jews in a 'double mirror', in the Law, properly so called, and in the kingship. Just as 'The Law was given, not to imprison the ancient People within itself, but to foster the Hope of Salvation in Christ until his Coming' (title of chapter vii), so also it was, as St Paul put it, 'our schoolmaster to bring us to Christ' (Gal 3:24). Calvin saw the Jews as in a state of childhood, needing all sorts of elementary aids, like the pictorial images of sacrifices and the priestly vestments. But all these, sometimes obviously, sometimes obscurely, prefigure Christ, the Mediator between God and men. Thus they both point forward to him and are at the same time valid Sacraments of his saving work.

As for the moral Law, it has its end, as St Paul says, in Christ. This, not in the sense that the moral commands are abrogated, but in that their teaching of righteousness is ineffective until Christ bestows righteousness by imputation and regeneration. In addition, the moral Law was given to make men aware of their sin and so drive them to Christ their Redeemer. It is this aspect that Calvin now emphasizes.

The Law makes men inexcusable (that strain again!). It demands complete and unswerving obedience. If any man fulfilled such obedience he would have eternal salvation, for so God promised. But it is precisely here that the weakness of the Law lies; its weakness in face of man's inability to obey its demands. It is not in man to keep the Law, and he is, therefore, excluded from life and laid under the Law's curse. This is not simply a fact of experience; it must happen: 'I do not speak only of what comes to pass, but of a necessity' (vii.3, 329^{25-26}). The demands of the Law are unattainable. All that is attainable is the fulfilment of the threats for non-compliance. Is, then, God mocking us when he promises so much good on condition that we keep the Law that we cannot keep? No, for in Christ God himself supplies what is lacking in us. He keeps the Law for us and gives us his obedience as a blessing.

But is it really impossible to keep the Law? Jerome anathematized the thought.[3] Calvin defines what he means by 'impossible'. Without going into the many kinds of impossibility, he says he means that which never has been and which God's ordination and decree prevent from ever happening. None has ever perfectly kept the Law; Scripture says that none ever will.

To clarify the statement he looks at the office and use of the moral Law under three aspects: first, by showing that righteousness is acceptable to God, it informs, convicts and condemns man of unrighteousness. Confronted by the Law, we see the truth about ourselves. Hence the Law is a mirror to show man his true appearance in God's eyes, so that

> naked and empty they may flee to his mercy, rest completely in it, hide themselves in it, and grasp it alone for the righteousness and merits which are set forth in Christ for all who long for and look for that mercy with true faith. In the precepts of the Law God is the rewarder only of perfect righteousness, and this we all lack. On the other hand, he is the severe Judge of all sins. But in Christ his face shines full of grace and softness even towards wretched and unworthy sinners. (vii.8, 334^{17-25})

Secondly, the Law restrains and deters from evildoing. This brings no credit to the one so restrained, for it is not a free and voluntary obedience, but simply a fear of punishment. In the effect, it even makes a man worse, in that he is resentful of God's restraint. The restraining is necessary for the sake of society but it is also related to salvation, for it keeps men from falling away utterly and becoming altogether careless about righteousness. 'All who have lived in ignorance of God will confess that it happened to them in such a way that they were restrained by the bridle of the Law in some sort of fear and reverence towards God until, regenerated by the Spirit, they began wholeheartedly to love him' (vii.11, 337[19-22]).

Thirdly, and chiefly for believers, in whose hearts the Law is written, it has the twofold purpose of teaching and exhortation. Day by day they learn the Lord's will for them. They are like a servant already prepared to serve his master but who has yet to learn his ways, his likes and dislikes, so as to fall in with them. In addition, there is the need for exhortation to obedience in opposition to their own disobedient flesh. 'The Law is a whip for the flesh, which is like a slow and lazy donkey' (vii.12, 338[8-9]).

Chapter viii, 'The Explanation of the Moral Law', sharpens and elaborates the issue – that the Commandments are still in force for Christians, that they taught the Jews of old the nature of true *pietas*, and that by their failure to observe the Commandments the Jews were driven to the Mediator. The Ten Commandments say nothing different from the law written on the hearts of all men. This inward law will not allow us to sleep morally, but it is not strong and clear enough by itself. Hence the need for the Decalogue, which is both certain and clear, and carries the authority of God's will, which all men are bound to obey. It is no excuse to say that it is impossible for us to keep the Commandments, for this is our own fault. The obligation remains of obeying our Father.

Confronted by the Commandments, we learn how far we are from being righteous. Thus we are led to judgement, to the despair of ourselves, to the fear of eternal death and hence to God's mercy and help.

The Commandments have an inward as well as an outward reference. They are not perfectly kept unless they are kept inwardly, as Christ taught in the Sermon on the Mount. But how are they to be interpreted? Their simple face value is too narrow. Therefore they must be interpreted according to their meaning and purpose, so as to see what pleases and what displeases God. This leads Calvin to the consideration of the opposites; what is commanded implies something forbidden and vice versa. The opposite of stealing, for example, is not abstention from stealing but active giving. (This in contradiction to Aquinas, *Summa Theologica* Ia IIae, xcviii, 1.)

It is according to these principles that Calvin goes on to expound the Commandments in order. For reasons of space we cannot now follow him step by step. It will be sufficient to note that the positive opposite to the prohibition is usually stated first, to be followed by the negative and positive consequences. Thus the First Commandment, in Calvin's rendering, 'Thou shalt not have alien gods before my face': 'The purpose of this Commandment is that God wishes to be exalted alone among his people and to possess them entirely and of right' (viii.16, 357[13–15]). The negative: 'For this to come to pass, he commands us to be free from all *impietas* and *superstitio*, by which the glory of his Divinity is diminished or obscured' (viii.16, 357[15–17]). Then the positive precept: 'and for the same reason he demands that we worship and adore him with a genuine zeal for *pietas*' (viii.16, 357[17–18]).

We have to be careful not to lose the thread of the argument as we are carried through the Commandments. There is, of course, considerable ethical teaching, but this section is not intended as an 'ethics', a self-contained discipline within theology. Calvin's aim throughout is first to emphasize the doctrine of chapters i–v that man is a sinner, and secondly to draw out the relationship between the Law and Jesus Christ, who was both its author and its realization.

The purpose of the Law is 'the fulfilling of righteousness, to form a man's life to the pattern of Divine purity. For God so delineates his own disposition in it that if anyone displays in his actions what is represented there he will in some degree be manifesting the image of God' (viii.51, 390[16–20]). All the teaching of the Law is comprehended in the command, first given in Deuteronomy 6:4–5 and then endorsed by Christ in Mark 12:30, 'Thou shalt love the Lord thy God with all thy heart, with all thy soul, and with all thy strength' and the corresponding 'Thou shalt love thy neighbour as thyself' (Lev 19:18; Mark 12:31). The meaning is 'first, that our soul should be filled in every part with the love of God; and then that that love should spontaneously flow out to our neighbour' (viii.51, 390[31–33]).

There is little difficulty in the interpretation of the former, but the latter caused some problems to mediaeval theologians (e.g., Peter Lombard, *Sent.* Lib. III, Dist. xxviii), who took 'as thyself' to imply that we are to love ourselves and also to love our neighbours. For Calvin it meant 'that we must be ready to do good to our neighbour with no less eagerness, ardour, and trouble than to ourselves' (viii.54, 393[21–23]). The identity of the neighbour is resolved as the *alienissimus*, the most foreign person in any sense of the word 'foreign': 'we must turn our eyes first of all not to the man himself, whose appearance often elicits more of dislike than of love, but to the God who demands that the love we owe himself shall be diffused to all humanity. The perpetual principle is:

"Whatever the man is like, he is to be loved because God is loved" '
(viii.55, 394$^{5-9}$).

Chapter viii has shown that the Law is to be understood in the light of Christ. But it was still a part of the old Covenant and thus of the twilight world. The relationship between that world and the new Covenant will be clarified in the next three chapters.

The claim of the New Testament writers that the old Covenant, with the Law and the Prophets, was a preparation for God's decisive work of redemption in Christ was early challenged, notably by the Marcionites, for whom the Creator-God portrayed in the Old Testament was not the Redeemer-God of the New. This, like so many ancient heresies, surfaced again in the sixteenth century. Some Anabaptist groups regarded the Old Testament as a book for the Jews only and irrelevant for Christians.[4] There had also been a tendency in the Middle Ages to play down the validity of the Sacraments of the Law. And there was not a little confusion in Reformation circles about the relationship between the two Testaments. These are the main backgrounds to chapters ix–xi.

Calvin's first step is to point to a certain superiority of the new Covenant without denying the validity of the old. Hence the balance in the title of chapter ix: 'Although he was known to the Jews under the Law, Christ was at last manifested in the Gospel'. The first sentence seems to weaken the superiority into an equality: 'It was not in vain that God wished in former times to declare by offerings and sacrifices that he was the Father; not in vain that he consecrated to himself a chosen people. There is no doubt that he was known then in the same image in which he now appears to us in complete brightness' (ix.1, 398$^{11-14}$). But it is the word 'brightness' that is definitive here. In very many places Calvin makes a distinction between the obscure and shadowy world of the old Covenant and the bright light of the Gospel, usually adding the quotation from Malachi 4:2, 'The sun of righteousness will arise with healing in his wings'. The superiority lies in the degree of clarity.

The confusion among some Reformers on the relation between the Gospel and the promises of salvation in the Old Testament has to be resolved. Is there not Gospel in both Testaments? Calvin does not think so. He defines the Gospel as 'the clear manifestation of the mystery of Christ' (ix.2, 399^{26}). Although it is true that the term can be broadened to include all the signs of Fatherly love which God showed to the saints before Christ, strictly speaking it should be kept for 'the proclaiming of the grace revealed in Christ' (ix.2, 399$^{5-6}$). This does not mean, however, as Servetus inferred, that the promises, because they had been fulfilled in Christ, had ceased in the same way as the Law and that, therefore, Christians are already in possession of all that had been promised. They do indeed possess the promised things in Christ, but these are still hoped for, in the future, according to Romans 8:23–25.

Nevertheless, the relationship between the two Testaments could hardly be closer than Calvin saw it: 'The Covenant with the Patriarchs differs in no way from ours in substance and reality, so that the two are actually one and the same, yet they differ in their administration' (x.2, 404$^{5-7}$). In explanation he sets out three principles on the old Covenant. First, it is not true that the Jews were given or promised only earthly blessings, as is often held. They also were adopted into the hope of everlasting life and assured of their adoption by the Law and the Prophets. Secondly, the Covenant in no way depended on their merits, but only on the mercy of the God who called them to be his people. And thirdly, they were united to God through the one Mediator, Christ. The rest of the chapter argues from scriptural proofs and illustrations of the sameness of the two Testaments. So good a case does Calvin make that at the start of the next chapter he is driven to exclaim: ' "What then?" you will ask, "Is no difference left between the Old and the New Testaments? What is to become of all the passages in Scripture where they are contrasted as quite different?" ' (xi.1, 423$^{3-5}$). The difference lies, as he has already said, in the mode of administration. This can be seen under four, or perhaps five, aspects.

The first concerns the same point as before. The Jews were certainly promised heavenly blessings, just as are Christians. But the Jews were given these indirectly, under the form of earthly blessings, whereas Christians have them directly before their eyes as their hope.

The second difference is that the old Covenant was given in the form of types and figures of what was not yet a present reality, whereas the new revealed the reality itself: 'the old showed only an image and shadow of the body, the truth itself being absent; the new manifested the truth present and the substantial body' (xi.4, 426$^{11-13}$). The metaphors of shadow/light and shadow/reality are Calvin's usual way of explaining the relationship. Here it is shadow/reality. What he conceives seems to be that the various parts of the old Covenant are like the shadow of Christ cast on a wall. It is unmistakably Christ, but yet it is only his shadow. The new revealed the actual body whose shadow had been cast (not simply the human body of Christ, of course, but all that he was and did and suffered and taught). The Old Testament has to be interpreted on its own level as 'shadow', and not immediately Christianized as if the body were present (as Lefèvre d'Étaples, for instance, had done in his 1508 commentary on the Psalms). On the other hand, precisely because it is 'shadow' of what is to come and not some unrelated shade, it is to be interpreted figuratively and typically. For Calvin a type is an institution or person under the old Covenant which existed in order to resemble in some significant respect the Mediator who was yet to come. Thus, the sacrifices enjoined under the Law were types of the sacrifice of Christ on the Cross; David the king was the type of Christ the King. The consequence is that the old Covenant was in force only until the 'body' replaced its own 'shadow'. The old 'became new and eternal after it had been consecrated and established by the blood of Christ. This is why Christ calls the cup he gave to his disciples at the Last Supper the cup of the covenant in his blood – to signify that the truth [i.e., the reality as opposed to the shadow] is genuinely consistent with God's covenant when it is sealed with his blood, and by that truth it becomes new and eternal' (xi.4, 427[28–33]).

3 THE MEDIATOR

As we come to the plain manifestation of the Mediator who had been known under shadows and types in the old Covenant, the imagery of obscurity and brightness is left behind, replaced by the history of the Son of God becoming man and acting as Mediator between God and men.

It would be a misunderstanding to treat this chapter xii as the second part of a Christology, the first having occurred in I.xiii. Certainly, we have Christology in this chapter and, certainly, it corresponds to that earlier section; but what Calvin is now concerned with is the knowledge of God the Redeemer in Christ. Chapter xii begins to tell us how God in Christ redeemed man. Its title is: 'For Christ to perform the Office of Mediator he had to become Man'.

'He had to' (*oportuisse*). There was, then, a certain necessity in it. The second sentence puts it openly: 'If we ask about the necessity . . . ' (xii.1, 437[4–5]). In what way was it necessary for the Son of God to become man?

It was not a simple, absolute necessity. That is to say, it was not necessary to his being as the Son of God to become man; for, obviously, he was Son of God before he became man. Nor is it enough to say that the necessity lay in our being as humans, even as sinners. We cannot say that because all men were sinners the Son of God had to become man.

The necessity lay in the nature of the case. There was no other help for man. Or rather, since God's help could with justice have been withheld, it lay in the love and mercy of God in face of man's plight. But again there must be care. We are not to imagine God being overruled by a quality called 'love', which would then be a God above God. Hence Calvin places the necessity in God's decision when faced with man's sin. The case of sinners is hopeless; we are barred from fellowship with God and therefore from life. God could destroy or he could show mercy. He determined to show mercy, and that by coming in person to save us. It is in this sense of necessity that 'the Son of God had to become Emmanuel for us, that is, God with us' (xii.1, 437$^{17-18}$).

But we can also point to a necessity in the nature of the task and of its performer. The task was not to make men into better or even perfect men, but into God's children, to make 'heirs of Gehenna into heirs of the heavenly kingdom' (xii.2, 438^{24}). This was possible only by the exercise of the reverse condescension, by the Son of God becoming man: 'because the Son of God by nature prepared for himself a body from our body, flesh from our flesh, bones from our bones, that he might be the same as us' (xii.2, 438^{28}–439^{1}). This union meant his 'taking what is ours and transferring to us what is his' (xii.2, 438^{26}), 'taking what is his by nature and making it ours by grace' (xii.2, 438$^{26-27}$).

His task was to swallow up death. Only life could do this. Only righteousness could conquer sin. Only the supreme Lord could destroy the devil. But who possesses life, righteousness, supreme Lordship, except God? 'Therefore the most merciful God made himself our Redeemer in the person of his only-begotten Son when it was his will that we should be redeemed' (xii.2, 439$^{18-20}$).

The initial chief part in reconciliation was, therefore, that the Son of God united himself with men so that he and they should have all things in common. The way in which the Mediator removes sin, the barrier to reconciliation, is the second part. Calvin treats this in terms of the Pauline doctrine of the first and second Adam: 'man, who destroyed himself by his disobedience, owed it to offer obedience as the remedy, owed it to make satisfaction to the judgement of God, and owed it to pay the penalty for sin' (xii.3, 439$^{22-24}$). This the first Adam and all his descendants could not do.

'Therefore our Lord appeared as true man, put on the person of Adam, took his name [*Adam* = 'man' in Hebrew], to take man's place in obeying the Father, to present our flesh as the price of satisfaction to the just judgement of God and in the same flesh to pay the penalty which we had deserved' (xii.3, 439$^{24-28}$). Yet this cannot be seen only in terms of Christ's flesh. It concerns his two Natures. As God, he could not experience death. Therefore, if he was to die he must become man. As man he could not overcome death. Therefore, he had to be God.

Calvin has not been considering the humanity of Christ in the abstract, but as the condition for executing the office of Mediator. One of his judgements on scholastic and contemporary Roman theology was that it was weak in its Christology; not in the sense that it was heretical, but in that it was not applied to men and, therefore, became irrelevant. But Christ cannot be considered apart from his people, for he has bound himself irrevocably to them.

The positive teaching in chapter xiii (much of it is refutation of various heresies) is elementary. Christ was genuinely human, 'subject to hunger, thirst, cold, and other infirmities of our nature' (xiii.1, 448$^{13-15}$). In his commentaries on the Gospels he will extend these infirmities to psychological traits, that Christ was sometimes frustrated, unhappy, wanting affection, and so on.[5] In his case these were not sinful, because he had them completely under control. The term 'son of man' is a Jewish idiom to express his true humanity. He is the lineal descendant of Abraham and David through both Joseph and Mary. As man he is distinguished from all other men by his sinlessness. This, not because of the Virgin Birth (which Calvin holds, together with the perpetual virginity of Mary), but because at his conception he was sanctified by the Holy Spirit to be as man before the Fall.

A point of historical significance occurs at the end of the chapter when Calvin rejects the objection to classical Christology that 'if the Word put on flesh he was therefore shut up in the narrow prison of an earthly body' (xiii.4, 458$^{5-7}$). Calvin's reply is: 'although the infinite essence of the Word was joined into one person with man's nature, we do not imagine any confining. The Son of God descended from heaven so wonderfully that he did not leave heaven; he was willing to be carried in the Virgin's womb, to live on earth, and to hang on the Cross so wonderfully that he always filled the world as from the beginning' (xiii.4, 458$^{7-13}$). This point was later taken up by Lutheran opponents as evidence that he was creating a duality in Christ, the Christ of history and a separate Christ who sustained the universe. It became known as the *extra-Calvinisticum* – the Calvinist outside; i.e., a Christ outside Christ. From the next chapter we may gauge the truth of the charge.

That chapter, bearing the title 'How the two Natures of the Mediator constitute the [one] Person', is a strong assertion of the Chalcedonian position, particularly as drawn from the *Quicunque vult*, the so-called Athanasian Creed: 'who, although he be God and Man, yet he is not two, but one Christ; One, not by conversion of the Divinity into flesh, but by taking of the humanity into God; One altogether, not by confusion of substance, but by unity of Person. For as the reasonable soul and the flesh is one man, so God and Man is one Christ'.[6] The first paragraph of chapter xiv keeps closely to this statement. It starts out from John 1:14, 'The Word became flesh'. This is not to be understood, says Calvin, as a conversion of the Word into flesh or of a confused mixture. He chose for himself a place of habitation, a temple fashioned in the Virgin's womb.[7] The Word is related to the flesh, not by confusion of substance but by unity of Person. The Divinity and the humanity each retains its own character or property. But from these two is constituted the one Christ.

Calvin knew the danger of analogy from human to Divine – we saw earlier his distrust of Augustine's Trinitarian analogy. But here he cautiously accepts the analogy in the *Quicunque vult*. Man is composed of two *substantiae* ('essences' or 'beings'), which are not mixed so that neither retains its proper nature. The soul is not the body, nor the body the soul. Some things are applicable to either but not to the other; some to the whole but not to either separately. On the other hand, some properties of the soul are transferred to the body and vice versa. Yet there is the one man. Scripture bears witness to Christ in a similar way. Sometimes it refers to his humanity alone or to the Divinity alone that which does not apply to the other. Sometimes it transfers to the one what is true of the other. This is a figure of speech called *idiomatōn koinōnia*, usually known in its Latin form as *communicatio idiomatum* – the communication of properties.

Using this traditional method, Calvin quotes passages of Scripture relating to Christ's Divinity and others on his humanity. Thus, John 8:58, 'Before Abraham was, I am', refers to Christ as God, whereas Luke 2:52, 'Jesus increased in wisdom and stature', refers to him as man. *Communicatio idiomatum* is to be seen in, for example, Acts 20:28, 'God hath purchased the church with his own blood', or 1 Corinthians 2:8, 'the Lord of glory was crucified'. Passages true of him both as God and man are, for instance, where he calls himself 'the light of the world' (John 8:12) or 'the good shepherd' (John 10:11).

It is consonant, therefore, that Calvin should reject the ancient Christological heresies of Nestorianism, with its separating of the two Natures, and Eutychianism, with its minimizing of their distinction. But he is, he says, not so worried about these ancient heresies as by a monster who has emerged in his own day, and who is no less deadly than the heretics of old. This is Servetus, who destroys the distinction between the two Natures, thus making Christ a mixture of two elements, Divine and human, and not the one God–Man. To both Servetus and the early heresies Calvin opposes the Christology of the orthodox Councils: 'The definition of the Church stands firm. Christ is to be held the Son of God because he who was the Word begotten of the Father before the ages took human nature upon himself by hypostatic union. And by hypostatic union the old writers meant a union that constituted one Person out of two Natures' (xiv.5, 465$^{2-6}$).

Having stressed that the understanding of the incarnate Christ must be in terms of his Mediatorial office, Calvin gives content to this office in chapter xv. It is threefold, corresponding to his anointing as Prophet, King and Priest. The technical name for this is *munus triplex*, 'the threefold office'. The basis for the doctrine lies in the scriptural witness to Christ. We see him in the Gospels as Teacher or Prophet. We see him in Hebrews especially as Priest. And in many places he is declared to be the King. In the early Church the Priesthood and Kingship were often conjoined as a twofold office. Later all three were seen as a threefold office, although the twofold was the more usual. Calvin kept to the twofold in the 1536 and 1539 editions of the *Institutio*, but added the third in 1545. (It is worth noting that in his commentary on Hebrews he keeps to a twofold office, Prophet and Priest.)

First to be emphasized, however, is the objective reality of Christ. We may have the name 'Christ' on our lips, but envisaged may be either some figure of our own inventing or an empty Christ without power. Who, then, is Christ? He is the Anointed one, the Messiah or Christ, anointed to those offices which in the Old Testament demanded preliminary anointing, prophecy, priesthood, kingship. Christ's chief office was as King, although this does not exclude the others.

Christ the Prophet, or Teacher. Calvin does not intend this in the sense of a mere educator of those who needed only to be taught because they were ignorant. Christ's prophecy consisted in the proclamation of the Gospel, and the content of the Gospel is himself, the gift of God: 'He was anointed by the Spirit to be the herald and witness of the Father's grace' (xv.2, 473[17-18]). At the same time we are brought back to the first sentence of the *Institutio*: 'Well-nigh the whole sum of our wisdom . . . consists in these two parts, the knowledge of God and of ourselves'. This now receives its full meaning: 'Christ's prophetic dignity has this purpose – that we may know that all the parts of perfect wisdom are contained in the sum of the doctrine which he taught' (xv.2, 474[15-18]). This is the wisdom revealed to the Old Testament Prophets, that is, God's purpose as Creator and Redeemer in Christ. Christ was not, however, simply one in the line of Prophets bearing witness to a wisdom that was not their own. The Word who became flesh was Wisdom himself. His prophecy was the full revelation of the wisdom which had been shown in figures and types.

Here the unity between Christ and his people is brought into the foreground. The unity is such that Christ must never be thought of as an individual, as what Calvin called 'a private person'. All that he was and all that he did was for his people. His anointing to prophetic office was not only that he should be the Prophet, but also that his people should be prophets: 'he received anointing, not only for himself that he might carry out the office of teaching, but for his whole Body, that the power of the Spirit might be present in the continuing preaching of the Gospel' (xv.2, 473[20-22]).

Christ the King. First, the eternity of Christ's kingdom. The promises of perpetuity to David's kingdom apparently failed when it met its end at the hand of the Babylonians in the sixth century BC. But God's promises cannot fail. Therefore, these promises to David must be interpreted as looking forward to the real Kingdom of which David's was only a type: ' "Once have I sworn to David by my holiness, I will not lie; his seed shall remain for ever . . . " For there is no doubt that God there promised to be the eternal ruler and defender of the Church by the hand of his Son. For nowhere else than in Christ can be found the truth of this prophecy' (xv.3, 474[28-34]). Christ is the King who rules and guards his Church in the whole of its course while the world lasts.

As before, Christ and his people are united in this office. But now Calvin treats the subject eschatologically. That Christ is King should kindle in us the hope of blessed immortality. We should not expect earthly happiness because we are Christians. Here we live under the Cross. But Christ our King protects and guides us, and bids us lift up our hearts and minds to his future revelation and our possession of the kingdom.

There is also the sharing in his anointing. The anointing of Christ is with the Holy Spirit. 'Christ' means 'anointed'. At his Baptism he was anointed, not with oil, but with the Spirit. This is true also for believers. Indeed, they are called 'Christians' because of their anointing with Christ: 'For the Spirit chose to have his abode in Christ that from him might flow abundantly the heavenly riches of which we are in such need' (xv.5, 478$^{4-5}$).

Christ the Priest. The purpose of his priesthood is 'that he may be a pure Mediator, without blemish, who will reconcile God to us by his holiness' (xv.6, 480$^{2-3}$). Calvin's treatment of this part of the doctrine follows the same lines as in the others. First, Christ himself was anointed to this office that he might offer the sacrifice of himself for our reconciliation. Secondly, Christ receives us as his companions in this office. In ourselves we are defiled, but in him we are priests. This priesthood is regarded as applying to the Church as a whole and to individual believers. It is never independent but a sharing in Christ's priesthood. For believers the office of priesthood is fulfilled in their offering of themselves and all that they have to God and in entering the sanctuary (that is, God's presence) with prayers and praises.

4 CHRIST THE REDEEMER

At this point all the teaching of chapters vi–xv is concentrated into one strong stream. The opening sentence of chapter xvi sets the tone: 'What we have hitherto said about Christ should be referred to this one end, that we, who in ourselves are condemned, dead, and lost, should seek righteousness, freedom, life, and salvation in him' (xvi.1, 481^{23}–482^{1}). The chapter is concerned to show how this is possible: 'How Christ has fulfilled the Functions of Redeemer to win Salvation for us; in which are treated his Death and Resurrection and Ascension into Heaven'.

The two chapters (xv and xvi) are each a part of a whole on the understanding of the name 'Jesus Christ'. In the previous chapter, as we saw, the Mediator was considered under his name as Christ, the Anointed. Now attention is turned to 'Jesus', Saviour, the name given to him, not by man, but by the Angel: 'thou shalt call his name Jesus, for he shall save his people from their sins' (Matt 1:21). He is what his name signifies, and 'as soon as we turn away from him, however slightly, our salvation gradually slips away' (xvi.1, 482[12-13]). And thus Calvin, this man of the high Renaissance, is carried back into the adoration of the name 'Jesus' of the early Middle Ages. 'Jesu, the very thought of thee / With sweetness fills the breast' – a hymn that used to be ascribed to Bernard of Clairvaux, no doubt on the basis of such passages as the one Calvin now quotes: 'the name of Jesus is not only light but also food; it is also oil, without which food is dry for every soul; it is salt, without which whatever was offered would be tasteless; it is honey in the mouth, melody in the ear, rejoicing in the heart, and at the same time, healing medicine' (xvi.1, 482[15-20]). This is the language of devotion. When theological explanation enters, as enter it must, the devotion is not discarded but continues to inform the doctrine. We may treat this quotation from Bernard as the key signature to the music that follows.

In what sense is Jesus the Saviour? To answer this Calvin echoes (and expects us to pick up the allusions) the burden of the early chapters of the *Institutio* on looking to God and looking at ourselves: 'from the sight of [God a man] descends to the examination of himself' (I.i.2, III.32[12]). So here: 'Since no one can descend into himself and seriously reckon what he is like without feeling that God is angry and hostile to him, it is necessary for him to have a way of appeasing him' (xvi.1, 483[6-8]). As sinners, we are aware of God's wrath and of his curse on those who transgress his Law.

From considering this, however, Calvin turns aside to address a rather obvious problem. God sent his Son into the world to be the Saviour. But now it is said that God is angry and hostile. To reconcile these two things a threefold answer is given.

First, language of this sort is an accommodation to our understanding and is intended to make us feel our misery apart from Christ: 'Since our mind cannot seize on life ardently enough or accept it with the gratitude we ought to have unless we are first struck and overwhelmed by fear of God's wrath and the horror of eternal death, we are taught by Scripture (*sacra doctrina*) to see that apart from Christ God is, so to say, hostile to us' (xvi.2, 484[11-16]). Nevertheless, although an accommodation, it is not untrue. We are sinners and God will not love the sin that is in us. Calvin does not now degenerate into the facile statement that God hates the sin but loves the sinner, for, as we have seen, men are totally sinners. Therefore, how can God love the sinner?

Answer: he does not. Yet there is something in man that God loves – his own workmanship. Marred though this is by sin, it is not destroyed. Whatever man has made of himself, he cannot undo the fact that God made him: 'Although we are sinners by our own fault, we remain his creatures. Although we have chosen death, he made us for life' (xvi.3, 484$^{27-30}$). So far as we are concerned, God was moved by his mere love and mercy to receive us into his grace. But he cannot accept us as sinners, because even our creatureliness, in itself acceptable to him, is perverted by sin. Hence, 'so long as we remain sinners, [God] cannot accept us in our entirety' (xvi.3, 484$^{32-33}$). By the sacrifice of Christ God does away our sin, and this because he loves us as his creatures. God's love precedes our turning to God and Christ's sacrifice. Thus the order: 'It is because he first loved us that he afterwards reconciled us to himself' (xvi.3, 484$^{39-40}$).

God reconciled us to himself. Elsewhere Calvin will say that Christ reconciled God to us (e.g., 480^3), so that he is no longer speaking of a change in man to render him acceptable to God, but of the wrath of God having to be appeased by the priest bringing a *piaculum*, an expiation, by Christ offering the sacrifice of his own life. Thus it means a change in God's attitude towards us. In the end Calvin falls back on a quotation from Augustine: 'In a wonderful and Divine way he loved us even when he hated us' (xvi.4, 485$^{31-32}$).

We return to the original question: 'How has Christ abolished sins and removed discord between us and God and acquired the righteousness which makes him gracious and benevolent towards us?' (xvi.5, 485$^{37-39}$). The answer is, 'by the whole course of his obedience' (xvi.5, 486$^{1-2}$). It is the obedience of Christ to the Father which is the heart of Calvin's doctrine here, with the basis of Romans 5:19, 'For as by one man's disobedience many were made sinners, so by one man's obedience many will be made righteous'.

We notice that it is 'the whole course of his obedience', not only his death. On the other hand, Scripture often ascribes the winning of salvation to the Cross, and Calvin points to several passages. But the Apostles' Creed passes over at once from Christ's Nativity to his suffering under Pontius Pilate. Karl Barth criticized Calvin for precisely this moving from the Birth to the Cross;[8] but unjustly. It is quite clear that for Calvin salvation is won by 'the whole course of Christ's obedience', with the Cross as the culmination, as the supreme test of his obedience.

In the *Institutio*, but even more strongly in the commentaries on the Gospels, Calvin stresses the terror Christ felt, the horror of the judgement of God he was to undergo, the human desire to escape, the struggle he had with himself to overcome his human weakness. In the *Institutio* it causes Calvin to burst out with: 'This was the extraordinary and incomparable proof of his love for us, that he wrestled against a terrifying dread and in the midst of frightful torments threw off all care for himself that he might think only of us' (xvi.5, 487[4–6]).

As we said in the Introduction, Calvin has followed the Apostles' Creed throughout, but mainly tacitly. At this point, however, it surfaces and he expressly expounds it for the rest of chapter xvi. The Creed relates the sum of the history of Christ: 'suffered under Pontius Pilate, was crucified, dead, and buried, he descended into hell; the third day he rose again from the dead; he ascended into heaven and sitteth on the right hand of the Father; and from thence he shall come to judge both the living and the dead'. Calvin expounds each event as having a heavenly counterpart or as a sort of enacted symbol. Taken together they compose the one event of salvation and reconciliation.

Suffered under Pontius Pilate. Christ was judged by the Roman governor. The judicial form is significant. He did not die in any extra-legal way; his throat was not cut by bandits, he was not lynched by a mob. He was 'put on trial in a criminal court; he was charged and accused by witnesses; he was condemned to death by the mouth of a judge' (xvi.5, 488[16–17]). Even the circumstances of his death, therefore, corresponded to its eternal meaning as his trial and condemnation at the judgement seat of God in order that we might be acquitted: 'This is our acquittal – that our guilt . . . is transferred to the head of the Son of God' (xvi.5, 489[16–17]).

The symbolic nature of Christ's death continues in the cruci- fixion, in that 'hanging on the tree' was accursed by God, according to Deuteronomy 21:23 and Galatians 3:13. He suffered the curse of God to show that God's curse on our sin was lifted from us and transferred to him. This is illustrated by the Old Testament concept of the sin-offering, *ash*^{e}*moth*, which signifies both sin itself and the offerings and sacrifices for sin. The sufferings and death of Christ were not merely foreshadowed by but were the archetypes of the legal types and figures. Calvin describes the sin-offerings and Christ's death as *katharmata*. This is a word he uses in the comment- ary on 1 Corinthians 4:13 to explain 'we are become as the refuse of the world'. It 'signifies a man who was set apart under official curse for the expiation of a city. Such men, by receiving into themselves whatever was criminal and sinful in the city, cleansed the rest of the people and so are sometimes called in Greek *katharmoi* but more often *katharmata*.'[9] Christ was the *katharma*; he was consecrated and set aside by God for this purpose; he was officially cursed by God in the form of his death; he received in himself the sin of all the rest; and the rest of the people are cleansed. Yet the curse and sin were not triumphant over Christ, destroying the *katharma* who bore them. On the contrary, 'in submitting to [the curse], he crushed, broke, and scattered its whole force' (xvi.6, 490[27–28]).

He was . . . dead, and buried. 'Here again we have to see how Christ substituted himself in our place in order to pay the price of our redemption' (xvi.7, 491[11–12]). But now the 'how' somewhat changes its character. We are not given a rational explanation of how Christ was the substitution for sinners, but rather a few comfortable words on what it means for us. By dying he brought to pass that we should not die eternally. By his death he brought us life. By his union with believers, in his death he put to death their earthly members and killed their 'old man'. United with him, we share in his burial; that is, we are buried to sin. Thus there is 'a double blessing in the death and burial of Christ – liberation from the death to which we were enslaved and the mortification of our "flesh"' (xvi.7, 491[38]–492[2]).

Calvin was aware that the next clause, *he descended into hell*, was absent from earlier forms of the Apostles' Creed, but thought the concept necessary in that 'it contains the not-to-be-rejected mystery of something extremely useful' (xvi.8, 492[17–19]). It is true that the clause can be taken to mean that Christ was buried or, with more probability, that he descended to the place of spirits departed. But Scripture gives a better explanation: 'Nothing would have been done if Christ had died only a physical death. It was necessary also that he should feel the severity of the Divine vengeance so as both to undergo as substitute (*intercederet*) his wrath and to satisfy his righteous judgement' (xvi.10, 495[4–7]). On the Cross Christ 'fought hand to hand' against the forces of hell and all the horrors of eternal death. It means that 'he bore that death which is inflicted on sinners by the wrathful God . . . He was subjected to an invisible and incomprehensible judgement before God' (xvi.10, 495[17–23]). Therefore, Christ suffered not only in his body but also in his soul, which endured 'the fearful torments of condemned and lost man' (xvi.11, 495[26–27]). It is out of these torments that he cried, 'My God, my God, why hast thou forsaken me?' – 'a cry wrung from the anguish of his inmost soul' (xvi.11, 496[16]). But again the note of triumph – *Christus victor!* 'And so, by fighting hand to hand with the power of the devil, with the horror of death, with the pangs of hell, he won the victory over them and triumphed, so that now in our death we should not fear those things which our Prince has swallowed up' (xvi.11, 497[4–7]).

On the third day he rose again from the dead. The Cross and the Resurrection must always be kept together. Yet Scripture differentiates between their effects. By the death of Christ sin and death are abolished. In the Resurrection righteousness is restored and life raised up. It is through the Resurrection that the death shows its power and efficacy to us. As with the other clauses, Calvin points to the significance of the Resurrection for us. Through it we are called to strive after newness of life and mortification of the 'old man'; we are born again to righteousness; and we are assured of our own resurrection.

He ascended into heaven. The Ascension must be joined to the Resurrection; but it was now that Christ brought in his Kingdom. The main point that Calvin makes, however, is that 'he ascended that he might fill all things' (Eph 4:10). Christ went away, not to withdraw his presence, but to rule the universe more immediately. It is by the gift of the Holy Spirit that the risen and ascended Lord is present and fills all things: 'his promise to be with us even to the end of the world he fulfilled by his Ascension, in which, as his body was raised above all the heavens, so his power and efficacy are spread and proclaimed beyond the utmost bounds of heaven and earth' (xvi.14, 502[14–18]).

And sitteth on the right hand of the Father. This, says Calvin, is an image taken from the custom of rulers (he is plainly thinking of Roman courts), who had an *assessor* or assistant to whom judgements could be referred. Hence Christ's Session is a way of saying that 'he had been invested with the dominion of heaven and earth and had solemnly entered into the possession of the administration committed to him' (xvi.15, 503[10–11]).

What do the Ascension and Session mean for believers? First, Christ entered into heaven, not as a 'private person', but as the Head of his people, 'in our flesh, as if in our name' (xvi.16, 503[32–33]). Hence we not only look forward to the enjoyment of heaven, but already possess it in Christ, with whom we are united. Secondly, he is in the Father's presence as the continual Advocate and Intercessor for us sinners, or, in metaphor, 'he turns [the

Father's] eyes to his own righteousness, so as to avert his gaze from our sins' (xvi.16, 504$^{6-7}$). Therefore we have assurance and confidence before God. And thirdly, because he is ascended he bestows the power of his Spirit and all his gifts. 'He sits on high so that, having poured out from thence his power upon us, he may quicken us to spiritual life, sanctify us by his Spirit, furnish his Church with various gifts and graces, keep it by his protection safe from all harm, restrain by the strength of his hand the ferocious enemies of his Cross and our salvation, and, in short, that he may hold all power in heaven and in earth' (xvi.16, 504$^{15-21}$).

And he shall come again to judge the living and the dead. The Second Coming is the visible presence of Christ at the Last Day. He will come in the same physical form in which he was last seen by men at the Ascension, but with majesty and power, and accompanied by his heavenly hosts. That he will judge all men is full of comfort for believers. Who will be the Judge? The one who has redeemed us by dying and rising again for us. If he promises redemption now, we need not fear that he will condemn us then.

The chapter closes with another encomium on the Apostles' Creed as giving 'the whole history of our Faith in concise and distinct order. It contains nothing which may not be vouched for by substantial testimonies of Scripture' (xvi.18, 506$^{25-28}$). In a final passage of devotion he sends us to Christ alone, 'in whom are the treasures of every kind of blessing' (xvi.19, 508$^{15-16}$).

The next chapter concerns a point of great importance in Calvin's theology, but it appears in the form of a minor contemporary controversy. The point at issue was: is Christ God's instrument in effecting salvation, or is he himself the author of salvation?

Criticism had been levelled against Calvin, among others, for speaking of the *merits* of Christ. 'Merits' was a highly suspect word, redolent of Rome. The critics preferred to say that redemption is through the mere grace of God and that Christ was the instrument God used to effect redemption. Since grace is the total opposite to merits, it is clear that one cannot speak of Christ's merits. Calvin's reply is first to agree that redemption is entirely of grace. Even Christ himself as a man depended on God's grace and not on merits. But secondly, we have said already that the Atonement was a matter of the obedience of Christ. This obedience was the satisfaction that he made for sin and the paying of the penalty for sin. But what is this but saying that Christ deserved salvation because of his obedience? But he deserved it, not for himself, but for us. Thirdly, on the question of whether salvation is through Christ or in Christ, the answer must be the latter. Atonement means that Christ has won, merited, eternal life and all blessings by his obedience. He both possesses them and shares them with his people. Because he is one with them, what is his becomes theirs. Hence we must speak not only of the grace of God but also of the grace of Christ, a phrase immediately taken up in the title of the next Book.

Notes

1   See T. F. Torrance, *Calvin's Doctrine of Man* (London, 1949).

2   Peter Lombard, *Sent.* Lib. II, Dist. xxv.9: PL 192, 708.

3   Jerome, *Against the Pelagians*, I.10 and III.3: in Library of Nicene and Post-Nicene Fathers, pp. 452, 473.

4   See W. Balke, *Calvin and the Anabaptist Radicals* (Grand Rapids, 1981), pp. 309ff.

5   *Harmony of the Gospels*, CO 45; ET (Edinburgh, 1972), III, pp. 147–8.

6   H. Denzinger, rev. A. Schönmetzer, *Enchiridion Symbolorum* (Freiburg, 1965), p. 42, Sentences 34–37.

7   Not as in Library of Christian Classics, which makes the Virgin's womb the temple.

8   K. Barth, *Credo* (London, 1937), p. 73.

9   *Commentary on 1 Corinthians*, CO 49.370–371; ET (Edinburgh, 1960), p. 95.

Part Three

The way we receive Christ's grace

1 THE HOLY SPIRIT AND FAITH[1]

The Son of God has become man. The Mediator has reconciled God and men. Jesus, the Saviour, Christ the anointed Prophet, King, and Priest, has fulfilled the Law, suffered its penalties, and triumphed in so doing. This was the burden of Book II. But it is not left behind when that Book ends. As I have just said, the phrase 'the grace of Christ' is taken up in the title of the new Book: *The Way in which the Grace of Christ is received, what Fruits come to us from it, and what Effects follow*. The work of the Mediator is still the subject, but now it is asked how the dis-union between Christ and all others is reversed. Nor, although Book III corresponds to the credal clause 'I believe in the Holy Spirit', have we moved away from Christ to the third Person of the Trinity. The Spirit is the Spirit of the Father and of the Son. It is good Trinitarian theology that he appears only anonymously in the title as the Mode of reception, the Bearer of fruits and effects.

The grace of Christ and the mystery of the Spirit meet in the title of chapter i: 'The Things which have been said about Christ profit us by the secret Activity of the Spirit'. There is implied a certain distance between the Mediator and those he came to reconcile. 'Now we must see', begins the chapter, 'how the blessings which the Father bestowed on his only-begotten Son come to us' (i.1, IV.1[8–9]). The 'how' is shown by taking up even more emphatically the union of Christ with the believer: 'The first thing to be grasped is that as long as Christ is outside us and we are separated from him,

78

whatever he suffered and did for the salvation of the human race is useless to us and irrelevant' (i.1, 1^{10-13}). The union has two aspects, on Christ's side and on ours. On Christ's side the union is in one sense already effected in that he united himself with men by becoming man. But there is also the closer, more intimate union, in that he lives within the believer: 'To communicate with us what he has received from the Father he has to become ours and dwell within us' (i.1, 1^{13-14}). On our side, we must be engrafted into Christ.

The physical union is plainly common to all men. But since there are those who do not share the spiritual union, we are led on to consider the union effected by the secret activity of the Spirit. The doctrine of the Divinity of the Spirit in I.xiii.14–15 is now applied to the work of redemption. The Holy Spirit makes the saving work of the Mediator efficacious to men. He testifies inwardly to the meaning of the death of Christ; he applies the sacrificial obedience of Christ to men's hearts and so cleanses them from sin. Nevertheless, this must not be conceived as if the Spirit brought down these blessings from a Christ distant in heaven, for his is the activity of Christ himself in the uniting of himself with them: 'the Holy Spirit is the bond by which Christ effectually binds us to himself' (i.1, 2^{5-6}).

Calvin goes through the qualities ascribed to the Spirit in Scripture. He is 'the Spirit of adoption', he is life, water, oil, fire, and so on. All these correspond to his work in the believer. But his principal work is the giving of faith: 'Therefore, as we have said that perfect salvation is to be found in the person of Christ, so, in order that we may become partakers of it, he baptizes us in the Holy Spirit and fire, enlightening us to faith in his Gospel and thus regenerating us that we may become new creatures' (i.4, 6^{11-15}).

The subjects for the next two chapters have thus been introduced: first faith and then regeneration.

Chapter ii is entitled 'On Faith; in which its Definition is set forth and its Properties explained'. But before coming to the definition Calvin first clears away certain errors. First, it is not a mere opinion – 'what I think is . . . '; not even a persuasion of the truth or probability of something – 'I am pretty sure that . . . '. Nor is faith a general assent to the Gospel story. Its object is not 'God' in general, but Jesus Christ, the image of the invisible God. We must 'look straight at Christ' when we consider faith or we shall fail to understand it at all. Scholastic theology, says Calvin, is a terrible example and warning in this respect.

The schoolmen failed to concentrate on Christ as the object of faith, with the consequence that their doctrine of faith went quite astray. In the first place, it made it possible for them to invent the concept of 'implicit faith', which came to mean faith merely as the acceptance of authority, in contrast to 'explicit faith', a conscious and understanding assent to the truth. Whatever the original point of distinction, it provided an escape route for Occam (c. 1280–1349). When he had taken scholasticism to its conclusion of measuring Divine things by reason and had found this in fact an impossible course to maintain, he was saved from theological scepticism by retreating to the authority of revelation, that is, of revealed truths in the Bible. You cannot prove that God exists: therefore accept the fact as true on the authority of Scripture and the Creeds. You cannot prove that the substances of the bread and wine are converted into the substances of the Body and Blood of the Lord: therefore accept it on the authority of the Church.

Calvin returns to an earlier relationship of faith and knowledge. Cutting out the unscriptural and unpatristic notion which despairs of understanding, he binds faith and knowledge firmly together: 'Is this what faith means – to understand nothing so long as you submit your mind obediently to the Church? Faith is sited not in ignorance, but in knowledge, and that not only of God but of his Divine will' (ii.2, 10^{10-13}). Christian theology has been recalled to Clement of Alexandria: 'Now neither is knowledge without faith nor faith without knowledge'; and Cyril of Jerusalem: 'Faith is an eye which enlightens every conscience and imparts understanding'; and Augustine: 'We believed that we might know'.

But there is more to be considered here. Calvin was concerned to show that faith was not only subjective or mainly subjective but thoroughly objective; not simply an inward state of mind or heart but a relationship, and that the special relationship with the God for us, Christ. 'Implicit faith' is not only a denial of intellectual knowledge but also of this relationship.

Calvin can now (ii.6) begin to build up his definition. The object of faith is Christ, we have said. But, more precisely, it is Christ 'clothed with his Gospel' (ii.6, 13^{16}). For the only way we can in practice know anything about Christ is through what is told us in the Gospel about him. More than this, however; if Christ is clothed with the Gospel, it follows that he is present 'within' the Gospel, that is, he is its substance. As Calvin says later, there is a correlation between faith and the Gospel: 'Take away the Word and there is no faith left' (ii.6, 14^{27-28}). The first piece of the definition can therefore be stated: 'Faith is the knowledge of the Divine will towards us, perceived from his Word' (ii.6, 15^{10-11}).

But there are, in Scripture, many words of God which, although they must be accepted as declaring his will, are nevertheless condemnatory and frightening; whereas we are speaking about a faith that should seek God, not flee from him. Therefore, instead of the broad term 'the will of God', let us say 'God's goodwill or mercy', his goodwill towards us in Christ.

Thirdly, faith is a firm conviction, not something wavering and doubtful.

These three pieces are now fitted together to form the definition, that faith is 'a firm and certain knowledge of the Divine goodwill towards us, which is grounded on the truth of the gratuitous promise in Christ, both revealed to our minds and sealed in our hearts through the Holy Spirit' (ii.7, 16^{31-35}).

Calvin does not, however, go straight on to explain the definition, but has to clear up what he regards as another scholastic misunderstanding, the distinction between *fides informis* and *fides formata*; the first being a faith which is faith and nothing more, existing without any accompanying virtue, and the second a faith which is given fulfilment by the addition of love. Calvin would not allow that faith could exist without love (although it is not the element of love that is efficacious in the reception of salvation). Moreover, the faith envisaged, with or without love, was a *fides acquisita*, largely an assent to revealed truth in Scripture and tradition. Thus there was a possibility of a faith existing without love, a poor, weak faith, needing to be filled out with acts of love, but still faith. Calvin insists that the division is unreal. Faith and love go together. Even faith as assent to revealed truths is still the assent of the whole man, and not merely cognitive: 'it is of the heart rather than of the brain, a disposition (*affectus*) rather than an understanding' (ii.8, 17^{25-26}); 'faith can in no wise be separated from a disposition of *pietas*' (ii.8, 18^{17}). It is unthinkable that one part of a man can be in a true relationship with God while another is totally unaffected by him. Faith is the activity of the whole man. Faith and love are inseparable. Take away love and what is left is not faith at all.

We come at last to the explanation of the definition.

First, *faith is knowledge*. But it is not such knowledge as is concerned with sensory perception. This is not to deny the reality of the activity called 'knowing God'. Man himself really engages in this activity. But the object of this knowledge, God in Christ, is unique, completely unlike all other objects of man's knowing. And since the nature of the knowing is determined by its object, the knowing is itself unique. Hence Calvin says: 'When we call it knowledge, we do not intend such a comprehension as is commonly possessed of things which fall under human sense. For it is so above such things that the human mind must exceed and rise above itself in order to attain it' (ii.14, 24^{34}–25^2). How it can still be a genuine knowledge we shall see later.

Secondly, *faith is a firm and certain knowledge*. Calvin is now thinking in terms of being sure that God is faithful and true, of being without anxiety whether God's attitude to us is one of goodwill. Two things are to be grasped here. We must have confidence in God's Word; for there can never be assurance while we are doubtful whether we know God's will or whether he will be true to his Word. Then there is the accepting of God's promise for oneself; for there can never be assurance while we think of God's will apart from ourselves. Put simply, it is not only that God loves the world, but that he loves me; not only that Christ died for sinners, but that he died for me. The confidence and assurance, however, are not placed in faith itself; but in the object of faith, God's grace in Christ. To trust in our faith is vainglorious and doomed. Even in earthly affairs the power of faith lies in its object. All the faith in the world in an untrustworthy man is worth nothing. The most meagre faith in a trustworthy man is abundantly justified.

It is true that the believer still has doubts and assaults on his faith. 'When we teach that faith should be sure and secure we are not imagining a certainty untouched by doubt or a security unassailed by anxiety. Rather we say that believers have a continual fight with their distrust; and we are far from placing their consciences in some quiet retreat completely unmolested by any disturbance at all' (ii.17, $27^{25–32}$). How, then, can we speak of assurance? Because the very nature of faith means that at heart believers are on the side of their faith and its object in opposition to their doubts and temptations. Calvin refers back to the beginning of Book II, where in chapters ii.27 and iii.1 he had spoken of the division of believers into flesh and Spirit (the last word deserves a capital, for what is at issue is not a general psychological distinction in the soul but the sanctification of man's spirit by the Holy Spirit). Believers experience this struggle between their 'flesh' and their faith, 'when the unbelief and distrust still clinging to the remnants of the "flesh" rise up to assail the inwardly conceived faith' (ii.18, 29$^{16-17}$). But it is the faith which in the long run is always triumphant.

Faith triumphs, however, not by its inherent strength but through that of its object, the Word of promise. In all assaults faith can hear and hear again God's promise and rest on it. Moreover, the believer is one with Christ. The common idea is that if we look to Christ, we have assurance, but if we look to ourselves, there is only despair. There is truth in this and Calvin can sometimes put it in this way. But it conveys a remoteness of Christ, whereas, if faith is union with Christ, the believer cannot be separate from him:

Christ has been so communicated to you with all his blessings that all that is his has become yours, that you are become a member of him, in fact one with him. Hence, his righteousness overwhelms your sins, his salvation wipes out your condemnation, he intercedes with his worthiness so that your unworthiness may not come into God's sight. It is certain that we must not separate Christ from ourselves or ourselves from Christ in the slightest degree. Rather we should hold fast bravely to the fellowship in which he has bound himself with us. (ii.24, 34$^{32-40}$)

Lastly, faith is *both revealed to our minds and sealed on our hearts by the Holy Spirit.* Although the Word of promise is from God and has his authority, we are sinners and blind to its truth. We call the truth untruth and untruth the truth. In itself the written or spoken Gospel is powerless. As Calvin says frequently in his sermons, it can beat on our ear-drums without any effect until the Spirit bores through those drums into our minds. And not only our minds, but also our hearts: 'what the mind has taken in must be poured across into the heart; for if God's Word flutters only in the upper reaches of the brain it is not being received by faith' (ii.36, 46$^{33-35}$).

All along it is a question of enlightenment. First, the Word itself comes from God as light into darkness. Then the Holy Spirit opens the ears to hear the truth, so to say, and teaches inwardly, and that not simply by way of education but by the illumination of minds and hearts to perceive the truth of Christ and accept it as one's own. Putting it another way, the Spirit gives a new mind which corresponds to the object of faith. Our old mind of sin and darkness is put to death with the crucified Christ and the new mind of faith is given in Christ risen and new: 'illuminated by [the Spirit] the soul receives, as it were, new eyes to contemplate the heavenly mysteries, by the splendour of which it was before dazzled' (ii.34, 45$^{23-25}$).

Calvin condemns the doctrine of 'moral conjecture', that is, assessing the presence of faith according to the goodness of one's life. If we consider our own characters and actions honestly we shall certainly conclude that our faith, if we have any at all, is hardly worth calling faith. But the correlation of faith is not with ourselves and our morality or piety but with God's promises in Christ, with the knowledge of God's goodwill towards us. This knowledge is revealed to our minds and hearts by the Holy Spirit. It is through him that we believe that we are the children of God (Rom 8:16). Were these things not so and were 'moral conjecture' true, where would be the confidence which the New Testament ascribes to faith?

Where also the hope? For it is clear that faith and eternal life are joined in the New Testament. If faith can look no further forward than today, there cannot fail to be fear that tomorrow the soul will be back in unbelief. But it has already been shown that faith rests on the promises of God in Christ. These are not for the moment but for eternity. The believer can be confident about his perseverance, not because of the staying power of his faith, but because the one in whom he believes is both willing and able to keep him and not let him go. 'For if faith is, as we have heard, a firm conviction of the truth of God, that it will not be able to lie to us or be in vain, then those who conceive this certainty will forthwith expect that God will perform his promises . . . Thus, faith believes that God is truthful; hope expects that in the course of time he will reveal his truth. Faith believes that he is a Father to us; hope expects that he will always act as such towards us. Faith believes that eternal life is given to us; hope expects that it will at some time be revealed' (ii.42, 53$^{2-6}$).

2 REGENERATION TO LIFE

The first part of the title of Book II has been fulfilled, and we come to 'the Fruits' of the grace of Christ. According to Calvin's understanding of Luke 24:47 and Acts 5:31, the effects of faith are repentance and the remission of sins. Therefore, he says, the argument I am pursuing demands that I begin with both simultaneously. This being physically impossible, a choice must be made between repentance (now called 'newness of life') and forgiveness (now called 'gratuitous reconciliation'). The choice falls on the former, in that it will be a better preparation for considering the other rather than vice versa.

Repentance does not precede faith. Nor does it merely follow it. It is the product of faith. There can be no question of penitence as a practical preparation for faith, as some Anabaptists and 'their fellow-travellers the Jesuits' prescribe. Calvin is also not satisfied with the traditional division of penitence into mortification and quickening. Mortification, or contrition, was thought of as a deep and sorrowful awareness of sin and God's judgement, and quickening was the joy which comes from faith in God's mercy in Christ, like a being raised to life from the dead. Calvin saw a similar weakness in the division of repentance into 'Legal' and 'Evangelical'. In the former the sinner is stricken with a sense of his sin and is unable to escape from his guilty conscience – examples were Cain (Gen 4:13ff.), Saul (1 Sam 15:24–30), and Judas (Matt 27:4–5). 'Evangelical' repentance is when a man is not only stricken with a sense of sin and God's wrath but also puts his trust in God's mercy – for example, David (2 Sam 12:1–14), or Peter (Matt 26:69–75 with John 21:15–19).

All this, says Calvin, is true enough, but the scriptural meaning of repentance has still not been explained. The Hebrew word translated 'repentance' means 'conversion' or 'return'. The Greek word means a change of mind or purpose. These provide the basis for Calvin's definition: 'It is a true conversion of our life to God, arising from a sincere and earnest fear of God. It consists in the mortification of our flesh and of the "old man" and in the quickening of the spirit' (iii.5, 60^{2-5}).

To explain the definition Calvin fastens on three points. First, by 'conversion to God' is meant a transformation of the soul and not merely of outward actions. The transformation consists in 'putting away what it had been' (its 'oldness', *vetustas*), or 'making a new heart for oneself', or 'circumcising one's heart'. Secondly, repentance proceeds from a serious fear of God's judgement. This is not identical with the first. The fear of judgement precedes repentance and produces it by bringing a man to sorrow for his sin and hatred of it. Conversion begins from this 'godly sorrow' which hates sin because it is displeasing to God. For the third point Calvin returns to *mortificatio* and *vivificatio*. 'Depart from evil, and do good' says Psalm 34:14. 'Depart from evil' – *mortificatio*, or 'putting to death'. 'It is a thing extremely difficult and hard to "put off" ourselves and to depart from our inborn character. Nor can the flesh well be thought to have perished unless whatever we possess of ourselves has been annihilated' (iii.8, 62^{18-21}); and again: 'we cannot be formed to the fear of God and learn the elements of *pietas* unless we are violently slaughtered by the sword of the Spirit and annihilated' (iii.8, 63^{1-3}). *Vivificatio* is expressed by 'and do good'. But it is not possible to do good unless the heart and mind have 'put on' a good disposition. And this comes to pass 'when, our souls having been washed by his holiness,[2] God so imbues them with new thoughts and affections that they can truly be regarded as new' (iii.8, 62^{28-30}).

At this point Calvin brings *mortificatio* and *vivificatio* into the sphere of the union of Christ with the believer. Christ's Crucifixion was, as we heard, the destruction of sin, his Resurrection the bestowing of new life. Therefore, 'if we truly share in his Death, our "old man" is crucified by its power and the body of sin is put to death, so that the corruption of our primal nature may no longer be vigorous. If we are partakers of his Resurrection we are raised to newness of life by it, corresponding to God's righteousness' (iii.9, 63^{7-11}).

Earlier we noticed that Calvin had substituted 'newness of life' for 'repentance'. This he now takes up: 'In one word I interpret repentance as regeneration, the only aim of which is that the image of God, defiled and all but destroyed by Adam's transgression, should be re-formed in us' (iii.9, 63^{11-14}). The image of God is here thought of as 'holiness and true righteousness'. Complete perfection in this world is not possible; the whole life of the believer is one of repentance, with a continual struggle against the remnants of sin in him. Here Calvin uses the traditional terms: 'all the more sensible writers agree that a live tinder (*fomes*) of evil remains in the regenerate man, continually throwing up desires (*cupiditates*) which entice and incite him to commit sins. They also confess that the saints are still kept entangled in the disease of coveting (*concupiscendi*)' (iii.10, 65^{17-21}). Calvin calls on Augustine and other fathers for support and finds the only difference between them and 'us' to be that Augustine did not regard *concupiscentia* in believers as sin whereas 'we' do. Not that all human appetites and desires are in themselves sin, for they are a part of man as God created him and could not be eradicated without man's humanity being destroyed. Yet they are in rebellion against God's will and ordering: 'we teach that all man's desires are evil and we charge them with sin, not in that they are natural but in that they are disordered; and they are disordered because nothing pure or sound can proceed from a corrupted and polluted nature' (iii.12, 68^{3-6}).

Calvin now goes on, in a way reminiscent of his sermons, to conduct an imaginary dialogue with those Anabaptists who hold that believers 'are restored to a state of innocence and need not be careful to restrain the desire of the flesh' (iii.14, 69$^{21-23}$).

Anabaptists: 'You must follow the leading of the Spirit; if he leads you, you will never go astray.'

Calvin: 'But what about choosing between disgraceful and honourable, good and evil, virtue and vice?'

Anabaptists: 'Oh! these are just distinctions which come from the curse laid on the old Adam. Christ has freed us from them now.'

Calvin: 'In that case there is no difference between fornication and chastity, truth and lying, straight dealing and crookedness.'

Anabaptists: 'No need to be afraid! The Spirit won't tell you to do anything wrong. Just be bold and let him guide you.'

Calvin's final reply is that there is only one Christ and one Spirit, the Christ and Spirit of the Scriptures (iii.14, 69^{22}–70^6). If we wish to follow the guidance of the Spirit, we must read what he has said in Scripture. 'For Christians the Spirit of the Lord is not the restless wild phantasm which [the Anabaptists] have dreamed up or borrowed from the inventions of others. Christians devoutly seek the knowledge of him from the Scriptures. There they learn two things – that he is given to us for our sanctification . . . and then that we are cleansed by his sanctifying in such a way that as long as we are shut up in the burdensome house of our body we are besieged by many faults and much weakness' (iii.14, 70$^{22-31}$). Yet Christians must not dwell on their wretched sinfulness to the point of despair, which is Satan's device to keep them away from God and his forgiveness. As Bernard told his brethren at Clairvaux, honey must be mingled with the wormwood; when they think of their own low estate they must also think of the Lord and his goodness.

When Calvin summarizes the fruits of repentance in terms of the Law we can see the necessity for the chapters on the relationship between the two Testaments in Book II. 'The fruits of repentance' are *'pietas* towards God, *charitas* towards men, and holiness and purity in the whole life. In short, the more anyone forces his life under the criterion of God's Law, the more sure indications of repentance will he display' (iii.16, 72$^{29-33}$).

Repentance begins in the heart, but shows itself in corresponding outward practice, in walking humbly and, so to say, in mourning attire. Shows of penitence are right; the penitent will use them to beat down the desires kindled by the tinder of sin. But the early fathers made too much of such exercises. Their over-emphasis on bodily discipline obscured inward penitence and they also went too far with their rigorous demands. In any case, these exercises are not strictly repentance, which is a turning to God.

We move on from repentance and regeneration to the life which is regenerated. This, says Calvin, is far too large a subject to treat thoroughly here. Readers who want to know more must go elsewhere for it, and especially to the sermons of the fathers. The passage in which he sets out his own intention is of great importance, not only here, but also for the whole of the *Institutio*:

> It will be quite sufficient for me to have shown a method by which a godly man may be led to the right goal in ordering his life, and to have prescribed briefly a sure universal rule by which he may well measure his duties. Perhaps there will one day be time for carrying out such a project – or I shall leave to others a task for which I am really not fit. My nature is to love brevity and perhaps if I wanted to speak more fully I might not succeed. For even though a more prolix way of teaching might be very commendable, I should scarcely like to try it. The nature of the present work demands that we should touch as briefly as possible on simple and straightforward teaching. (vi.1, 147$^{1-10}$)

For the moment Calvin's intention is just to place an aim before the Christian. First, Scripture exhorts us to love righteousness. It is true that philosophers do the same; but they can only tell us to live in harmony with our own nature. Scripture not only exhorts us to relate our life to God our Creator but also sets Christ before us as the pattern whose image we may represent in our lives. It is not a question of a perfect Christian life, but of having perfection as the goal to aim at and of gradually making progress until, after this life, 'we are received into full community with him' (vi.5, 150$^{38-39}$).

Secondly, a method for ordering our life must be prescribed. Although the Law is the most appositely arranged way, a more precise rule is provided in Romans 12:1–2: 'I beseech you therefore, brethren, by the mercies of God, that ye present your bodies a living sacrifice to God, holy and acceptable; and be not accommodated to the form of this world, but be ye transformed by the renewing of your mind, that ye may approve what God's will is'. This is summed up as: 'So the great thing is for us to be consecrated and dedicated to God so that we shall not think or speak or meditate or do anything save to his glory' (vii.1, 151$^{12-14}$). No longer our own but God's, we must abandon ourselves to him and utterly devote ourselves to serving him in everything. Such self-abandonment was unknown to the philosophers, who regarded virtue as the control of life by reason. Christian philosophy dethrones reason and makes it subject to the Holy Spirit, 'so that the man does not live, but bears within himself Christ living and reigning' (vii.1, 152$^{2-4}$).

This denial of self, *abnegatio nostri*, is the subject of chapter vii and is presented in the title as the *summa* or chief part of the Christian life. It consists in the extirpating of *cupiditas* with its desire for possession and adulation, and the eradicating of ambition, the desire for human glory, 'and other more secret pests' (vii.2, 152$^{14-15}$). Along with it goes a disinterested love of virtue.

Abnegatio nostri has a twofold reference; first towards our fellow men and then towards God. Far from loving our neighbour as ourselves, there is so much self-love in us that we exalt ourselves and despise all others. We magnify the good in us as if it were our own and not given by God, and we hide and minimize our faults and even cherish them as virtues. We refuse to see the good in others and magnify their faults. But our virtues are only a façade. When things go against us or we get upset, we show our true nature. Scripture tells us to humble ourselves, remembering that all our good comes from God and honouring the good he has given to others: 'you will never arrive at true gentleness and kindness until your heart is dispossessed of yourself and filled with respect for the other' (vii.4, 155$^{14-15}$).

Yet how difficult this is! It entails abandoning all consideration of ourselves, in a sense unclothing ourselves of ourselves. How can our nature agree to suffer long and be kind, not envy, not boast, not seek our own, and so on, as we read in 1 Corinthians 13? Yet this is what we are called to. Indeed, every blessing and virtue is given us, not for our own use only but to be employed for the good of the Church. We are stewards, acting for God.

What is more, there is no limit to such love of the neighbour: 'whoever the man now set before you who needs your help may be, you have no reason for withholding it. Say he is a foreigner; yet the Lord has impressed on him a mark which should be familiar to you . . . Say he is contemptible and worthless; yet the Lord shows that he is made worthy by the beauty of his image. Say that you have no obligations towards him; yet God as it were substitutes him in his own place and thus in him [the neighbour] you can recognize the many and great benefits by which he [God] has laid you under obligation to himself. Say he is unworthy of your taking the least trouble for him; yet the image of God by which he is commended to you is worthy for you to give him yourself and all that you have . . . You may say, "he has deserved very differently of me". But what has the Lord deserved? When the Lord commands that whatever sin the man has committed against you should be forgiven, he certainly intends it to be imputed to himself. Only if we proceed in this way can we arrive at what is not only difficult but completely against human nature' (vii.6, 156^{36}–157^{17}).

There is also the *abnegatio nostri* in regard to God, and this is the principal part. It is the resignation of ourself and all that we have to God's will. We have an infinite *cupiditas* for wealth, or honours, or power and all the frills that seem necessary for a fine life. We fear and hate poverty, obscurity, lowliness, and try to guard against them. The pursuit of the one and the fleeing from the other creates a life full of restlessness, planning and labour. The godly must follow quite another course. They must not seek anything that lacks God's blessing. They will not use any means they can think of to get rich or famous at the expense of their neighbour. They will not be greedy for wealth or fame or honours, but will be ruled by God's Word. If things do not turn out as they had planned, they will not be discontented but will accept God's will for them.

This attitude should be applied to all the accidents of life, sickness, war, terrible weather, houses destroyed by fire: 'whatever happens, he will accept with a quiet and grateful mind, knowing that it was ordained by the hand of the Lord, and he will not stubbornly resist the rule of him into whose power he has once for all surrendered himself and all that he has' (vii.10, 161^{3-6}).

The descent into abasement is an ascent to the Cross. 'The godly mind should ascend higher still', say the opening words of chapter viii (161^{18}). For, as the title declares, bearing the Cross is a part of *abnegatio nostri*.

Christ's call to his disciples is to a hard and toilsome life, to a lifetime of bearing the Cross. His own life was a perpetual bearing of the Cross and by this, as Hebrews 5:8 puts it, 'he learned obedience'. We should not expect or seek exemption from what he to whom we are united underwent. On the contrary, what strengthens and comforts us in all our tribulations is that we are participating in his sufferings and that, as his way to resurrection life led to the Cross, so is it also for us.

There is this difference, however. The only reason for Christ's sufferings was to elicit and demonstrate his obedience, whereas the purpose of our sufferings is also to show up our weakness and so drive us to calling on God for help. Believers experience the realization of God's promises when they patiently rely on his help in the midst of their troubles. And this looks forward also, so that they have the steadfast hope that he will be as faithful in the future as he is now and has been in the past. A further reason for our sufferings is to test out our patience and so train us to obedience. Not that God needs to learn whether we are obedient, for obedience is his gift in the first place; but in this way it is brought out into the open and not left lying inert within us. Afflictions show up a man for what he really is.

Although Calvin does not tell us explicitly what he means by the 'Cross' that we must bear, it becomes clear that it is first the ordinary sufferings which all men undergo – sickness, loss, death, and so on. Hence 'bearing the Cross' is a patient acceptance of the troubles of this life. We do not realize how necessary patience and obedience are until we consider how wild and undisciplined towards God is our flesh so long as it is indulged and treated gently. It is like a horse left idle and well-fed and, therefore, unmanageable when it comes to be ridden. God tames and curbs this vicious horse, the flesh, with the sufferings he lays on us. Or he is like a physician treating the sick, who need different treatment, different medicines. Some need a major operation, others the sixteenth-century equivalent of a couple of aspirins and a day in bed. The heavenly Physician treats some tender souls very gently, others, who need severity, more roughly. Yet none is left without treatment, for all are sick.

Bearing the Cross has a past as well as a present reference. It is not only to train us in patience and obedience but also to correct our past faults by the discipline of suffering. We should, therefore, cast our eyes over our past conduct. We shall certainly find that it needs to be corrected by unpleasant medicine. Yet the awareness of our failures is not the principal thing that suffering should bring, but the knowledge that our heavenly Father is correcting us for our good. 'Scripture teaches us that there is a difference between unbelievers and believers; the former, as slaves inveterately double-dyed in wickedness, only become worse and more obstinate under the rod; the latter, as free-born sons, make progress in repentance' (viii.6, 166^{6-9}).

There are also the special sufferings of Christians, sufferings 'for righteousness' sake'. Not just those who suffer persecution in defence of the Gospel, the martyrs of every age, but also those who quite simply stand up for what is right. It may be defending the truth, or it may be protecting the good and innocent against oppressors. If believers do this, they will incur hatred and opposition.

They should show their gratitude to God by receiving such persecution freely and gladly. It is not that they do not feel the pain of it. They are not unfeeling Stoics. And Calvin takes the opportunity to reject the Stoicism dredged up from classical times by the Renaissance and so attractive to the intelligentsia of the day. 'We have nothing to do with the iron philosophy which our Master and Lord condemned, not only by what he said but also by his example' (viii.9, 168$^{11-13}$). There is no need for believers to feel guilty when they feel ordinary human unhappiness and are not always completely patient and cheerful as these Stoics demand. Scripture teaches that what is praiseworthy is when believers are not broken by their suffering but rather turn to God for comfort and joy. Bearing the Cross is a matter of subjugating impatience and resentment and distrust instead of being overcome by them.

The philosophers inculcated patience also, but it is very different from Christian patience. For them suffering must be borne because it is necessary – what must be, must be. There is nothing else for the sufferer to do but be patient, apart from surrendering to despair. But Scripture teaches that nothing happens but by the Providence of God and that he works most justly. Hence the believer is not yielding to necessity but obeying God and acquiescing in his own good when he bears the cross: 'The Lord has so willed. Let us follow his will' (viii.10, 169$^{25-26}$).

The Cross, however, endures only in this life. Beyond are the resurrection and eternal life. To this we turn with chapter ix: 'On the Meditation of the Future Life'. The word *meditatio*, which in English sounds like a calm inward contemplation, commonly means 'preparation'. Another meaning is 'practice'. The three senses taken together will bring out different aspects of Calvin's thought here. The believer thinks about the future life. More, he prepares for it. More, he practises it in this life.

In the midst of all our troubles we must remember that they have this particular purpose of training us to despise the present life and so arousing us to the *meditatio* of the future. We are naturally at home in this life and cling to it. The Lord therefore needs to use the miseries of this life to teach us how unstable and fleeting and empty it is. We have only truly profited by 'the discipline of the Cross' when we have learned this lesson.

There is no halfway house: 'either the world must become worthless to us or it will hold us in the bonds of an intemperate love' (ix.2, 171$^{37-39}$). For the world is so alluring that we need to be called away from it or we shall be bewitched. Everyone is well aware, but too easily forgets, that man's life is only a mist and a shadow. Hence the need for God to train us by afflictions and for us to pay heed to him, despise the world and strive wholeheartedly towards the thinking, preparing for and practising the future life.

But despising the world does not mean hating it or being ungrateful for God's many blessings, but only that, while we are grateful, we should also realize the wretched state of things in this life. The only hatred we should feel towards it is because it keeps us liable to sin. Believers should view the present life as wretched, but be led on by this thought to desire the life to come. 'For if heaven is our homeland, what can the earth be but exile? If going out of the world is entering into life, what is the world but a sepulchre? To remain within it what but to be sunk in death? If to be set free from the body is to be released into perfect liberty, what is the body but a prison? If to enjoy the presence of God is the height of bliss, is that not to lack all misery?' (ix.4, 174$^{7-13}$). It is in comparison with the heavenly life that this is to be hated. But the ending is according to God's will and in his own time. Believers are like soldiers on duty; they must stay at their posts until their Captain moves them.

It is monstrous that professed Christians should tremble at the very mention of death. Certainly, it is fearful to our natural senses, but *pietas* overcomes the fear. By death the body is dissolved only to be restored at last to an incorrupt and heavenly glory; by death we leave the land of exile for home. This, Calvin says, is too big a subject to deal with here and he recommends us to read Cyprian's treatise *On the Mortality*. All he will now say is that none has made progress in the school of Christ but the one who looks forward with joy to the day of death and so to the final resurrection.

This scene is replayed. The next chapter is introduced with *simul*, 'at the same time'. We must certainly meditate on, prepare for and practise the future life; but the fact remains that we are still in this life. And 'if we have to live, we must also use the necessary helps of life' (x.1, 177$^{11-12}$) – and also enjoy the pleasures and delights of the earth.

Everything should be ordered by the measure which God prescribes in his Word. We should regard this present life as a pilgrimage by which we journey to the heavenly kingdom. Therefore, we should use the good things of this life so that they help and not hinder our journey. Some (Calvin is no doubt thinking of ascetics in the early Church, for he calls them 'in other respects good and holy men') allowed the use of earthly things only so far as was necessary to live. This was too strict, especially as their view of 'necessary' meant only what they could not do without, which came down to bread and water. At the other extreme there are, he says, some today who have become completely permissive and have no other standard than the individual conscience.

The principle he lays down is that the right use of earthly things is 'when they are referred to the end for which their Author himself created and destined them. He created them for our good, not for our ill' (x.2, 178$^{11-14}$). Why has God given us food? Not merely to keep us alive, but to give us pleasure. Clothes? Not only for decency and protection, but also for beauty and becomingness. The natural world of trees and their fruits? Not only for their usefulness, but also to please by their sight and delight by their scent. 'Is it wicked to be affected by their beauty or their scent? What! Did he not make a difference in their colours, so that some should be fairer than others? What! Did he not make gold and silver, ivory and marble handsome, so that they are precious above the other metals and stones? In short, did he not make many things agreeable to us in addition to their necessary use?' (x.2, 178$^{28-34}$).

Therefore, away with immoderate puritanism! Away with 'that inhuman philosophy' that would rob men of their senses and allow only what is entirely necessary. Yet, characteristically, Calvin at once warns us of the opposite extreme, everyone pleasing himself and enjoying not liberty but licence. All good things are given to us in order that we may know that God is their Author and so give him thanks. Where would be the gratitude in stuffing ourselves with food or getting drunk, so that our bodies and wits were not in a fit state to give thanks? Where the gratitude if our fine expensive clothes make us vain and contemptuous of the meanly attired?

There are two rules to observe. First, as 1 Corinthians 7:31 says, we should 'use the world as not using it'. In this, St Paul is not only telling us to abstain from excess, but also ruling out every care and affection that hinders our concentrating on the heavenly life. The second is to learn to bear poverty and failure as well as wealth and success patiently. If we have learned this we have profited well in the school of the Lord. To be discontented at one's lot is only the converse of the enjoyment of licence. The man who is ashamed of his cheap suit would only boast if he had an expensive one. What upsets the man who is discontented with his miserable meal is that he wants a feast; and if he had a feast he would abuse it intemperately. There is also this third rule, that God uses us as his stewards when he gives us his blessings; we must remember that we shall have to give an account of our stewardship.

Finally, God has allotted to each individual his own sort of life. These different kinds of life are called 'vocations', situations to which God has *called* us. 'Hence, the kind of life of each is like a soldier's post assigned by the Lord, so that he should not be driven about aimlessly through the whole course of his life' (x.6, 181$^{4-6}$). This calling of God is the beginning and foundation of well-doing in every part of life and our lives are best framed when they are directed towards this mark, so that 'there will be no work so dirty and mean but it is resplendent and very precious in God's eyes as you obey your calling in doing it' (x.6, 181$^{30-32}$).

3   JUSTIFICATION BY FAITH ALONE

As he embarks on the doctrine of justification (chapter xi, 'On the Justification of Faith, and first of the Definition of the Name and the Thing') Calvin takes particular care both to connect the doctrine with his general argument and also to explain why he deals with it after regeneration. The order he has adopted now compels him to recapitulate the teaching of the early chapters. The sum of it is that, possessing Christ by faith, we participate in him and receive a twofold grace – first, that we are reconciled and so have God as our Father instead of our Judge; and secondly, that we are sanctified by the Spirit and should practise innocency of life. Why treat the second part first? Because it is necessary to grasp that faith, the sole means of obtaining righteousness by God's mercy, is not idle in doing good works, and also to explain what those good works are. It would seem, then, that this ordering of the material was a response to the Romanist criticism that the Reformers conceived a faith empty of love and good works.

On the other hand, Calvin had laid himself open to attack from Lutherans as suggesting that good works, although produced by faith, can at least be considered before justification – a doctrine that could open the way for the old system of 'infused faith', 'formed faith' and 'merit from worthiness'.

However, if we take Calvin's explanation as genuine (as no doubt it was), it comes as no surprise to hear him say in Luther-like tones that justification by faith alone 'is the chief thing in the upholding of religion' (xi.1, 182$^{15-16}$). The word I have indeterminately rendered 'thing' is *cardo* ('hinge'), that 'on which everything else depends or turns'. If we want the Christian religion to survive and flourish, Calvin is saying, we must put justification by faith alone at the heart of it: 'For unless first of all you grasp where you stand with God and what his judgement on you is, you have no foundation on which your salvation may be established or on which *pietas* towards God may be raised' (xi.1, 182$^{17-20}$).

As this section on justification is one of the longest in the *Institutio* (chapters xi–xix), it will be helpful first to look at our way ahead. In chapter xi the first two paragraphs tell us what justification is; paragraphs 3–4 give the scriptural basis for the doctrine; paragraphs 5–12 contain a refutation of the German Reformer Osiander's doctrine and paragraphs 13–20 a refutation of the scholastic doctrine. At paragraph 21 Calvin returns to his definition and expounds it until the end of the chapter. Chapter xii impresses on us the seriousness of the matter, that we are on trial before the most high God. Chapter xiii sets out the points which theologians must always bear in mind, assert and safeguard – that God's glory shall not be impaired and that men shall have peace of conscience. Chapter xiv considers justification in practice, in that it is not only a matter of God's declaration in eternity or at the Cross, but also affects men on earth. Chapters xv–xvii declare that any human claim to righteousness is self-destructive in that God's glory is impaired and man has no peace of conscience. It leads to the question of rewards promised in Scripture, which is the subject of chapter xviii. Christian freedom is treated in chapter xix as an appendage to justification.

We must first look at Calvin's concept of justification, the general way in which he views it. As we do, we see that this is something he has been working up to all through the *Institutio*, and that the argument of Romans 1 – 3 has been the underlying theme.

Man is on trial. He attempts to justify himself by pleading ignorance of right and wrong, by pleading his human frailty, by pleading the bad example of the rest of mankind. He even accuses his Judge of unfairness. One by one his excuses are swept away by the clear testimonies of the Judge's published self-revelations. At last the man has no excuses left. He is *anapologētos*, without excuse, without a word to say in his own defence. What have made him so are the many possibilities he has had but not used – the awareness of God imprinted on his mind, the self-revelation of God in the creation, and, if he knows it, the Law or, if he does not, the law written in his heart.

This is the concept which lies behind and informs Calvin's doctrine. It is called 'forensic', and so it is. But this is such a law court as never was in the world. The Judge is also the Accuser. The Judge changes into the Father. The guilty man is judged righteous. The trial is not an example of the machinery of the Divine Law taking its course, but a confrontation with God's grace.

Now for the doctrine itself.

It is first necessary, says Calvin, to explain the terms 'to be justified before God' and 'to be justified by faith or by works'. A sinner can never be accepted by God, to whom all sin is abhorrent. Sin and God's goodwill are mutually destructive. What belong together are sin and God's wrath. Therefore, for a man to be accepted by God he must be righteous – that is, in complete agreement with God's good and holy will. If he is thus in himself, he is said to be justified by works. But if, as is indeed the case, he is not perfectly in agreement with God, then God is not well pleased with him but against him as one to be rejected. 'At God's judgement seat all sinners perish' (xi.2, 182^{32}). God, in whom is no falseness, cannot say of the sinner that he is innocent.

Yet Calvin will speak of the possibility of a man's being justified. How is this so? It is a possibility which resides not in the man, but in God. We may call it justification by Christ, or by mercy, or by grace, or by faith. They all say the same thing. 'To justify is therefore nothing else than to absolve the guilty man from guilt as if he were proved innocent. When God justifies us by the intercession of Christ he acquits us, not on account of our own innocence, but by imputing righteousness, so that we who are not righteous in ourselves are reckoned righteous in Christ' (xi.3, 184^{9-14}); and: 'He is justified by faith who, excluded from the righteousness of works, grasps by faith the righteousness of Christ, clothed in which he appears in God's sight not as a sinner but as righteous' (xi.2, 183^{5-7}).

It is not, however, a question of God's justifying man because his faith is a virtue pleasing to God and winning his favourable verdict for that reason. In the quotations just given Calvin at once replaces faith itself ('justified by faith') by faith seen in its reference to its object ('grasps by faith the righteousness of Christ'). We shall take up the point about being clothed in Christ's righteousness later.

We are brought to the main definition: 'We interpret justification simply as the acceptance by which God regards us as righteous whom he has received into grace. And we say that it consists in the remission of sins and the imputation of Christ's righteousness' (xi.2, 183$^{7-10}$).

It is at once plain that Calvin is talking of an act of God. In the definition God reigns as the Divine Subject: *God* accepts us; *God* receives us into grace; *God* regards us as righteous. Justification is initiated and carried through by God and by God alone. In this act there is no place for man as God's fellow worker.

The gravamen of Calvin's charge against the 'sophists' (the mediaeval scholastics and the current Romanist teaching culminating in Session Six of the Council of Trent[3]) was that they had not kept their gaze fixed on this truth. Indeed, 'the schools have continually wandered further and further astray until at last they have fallen into ruin and a sort of Pelagianism' (xi.15, 199^{29}–200^2), a charge, we may note, that had been levelled by more than one theologian during the past century. In Calvin's view they had taken the wrong turning by a misunderstanding of the nature of both faith and grace. Faith had been demoted into a belief that God will reward meritorious acts; it had not been put into absolute opposition to works. Grace had become the assistance of the Holy Spirit in the striving for holiness, instead of the imputation of free righteousness. The Romanists attacked the Reformers for using the expression *sola fide* – 'by faith alone' – on the grounds that it is not found in Scripture. This is literally true, Calvin admits; but the same thing is said in other words; for example, Romans 3:28, 'we conclude that a man is justified by faith without the deeds of the law' (Law here being taken for the moral as well as the ceremonial Law). But, it was argued, the faith of which Paul was speaking was 'faith working by love' (Gal 5:6) and it is the quality of love (thought of here as the fountain of all good works) which gives faith its power to justify. We have already seen that Calvin agrees that justifying faith is the faith that works by love, otherwise it would not be faith at all. But faith justifies 'because it brings us into communication with Christ's righteousness' (xi.20, 204^{21}).

Secondly, justification is *an acceptance*. Acceptance is the opposite to rejection. God rejects all that is in opposition to him. He accepts that which is in agreement with his goodwill, that which pleases him. Note that justification is not *by* acceptance; it *is* acceptance. And the sort of acceptance is shown in the next clause, 'received into grace'. Here grace is used in the sense of being favourable towards another. God takes into his favour the one who stands guilty before his judgement seat. This little phrase *nos . . . in gratiam receptos* denotes the miracle, the incredible reversal which is justification by faith alone. It denotes the unexpected and undeserved good pleasure of God.

'*God regards us as righteous*'. This is the explanation of 'acceptance', 'the acceptance by which God . . . regards us as righteous'. Thus it is not 'the acceptance in which God . . . makes us righteous'. But 'regards' is stronger than 'declares', and removes any suggestion that God should be acting a lie. Nor is he pretending. If he so regards the case, then so it is, for it is impossible that he should lie or be deceived.

Justification *consists in . . . the imputation of Christ's righteousness*. Imputation means reckoning to someone what was not his previously or inherently. Righteousness belongs inherently only to one, Christ. Therefore, 'we are reckoned righteous before God in Christ and outside ourselves – *in ipso et extra nos*' (xi.4, 185$^{17-18}$). To say that God imputes to the sinner Christ's righteousness means that he sees that righteousness as if it belonged to the sinner. He sees the sinner not in his naked sinfulness, but clothed in Christ's righteousness. God looks at a sinner. What does he see? Someone dressed in Christ's clothes. How strongly Calvin felt the force of this image comes out at the end of the chapter, where he quotes with approval a piece of spiritual interpretation by Ambrose. Jacob wishes to receive the blessing from his father Isaac. He therefore comes to him wearing the clothes of his elder brother Esau, with the scent, sweet in his father's nostrils, of the sheep upon them. In the same way, we must hide under the precious purity of our first-born brother, Christ, so that we may be accepted by our Father, God.

At this point Osiander has to be refuted. His starting point in justification is little different from Calvin's, the unity of Christ with believers. But he virtually ignored the manhood of the Mediator and taught that it was Christ's Godhood that becomes one with believers by infusion of the Divine essence. Calvin's objection (shared by many of Osiander's fellow Lutherans) was not only that this was a sort of Manichaeism, making God and men essentially one, but that it also diverted attention away from the Mediator: '[according to him] we are justified, not by the sole grace of the Mediator . . . but we become partners in the Divine righteousness when God is united with us substantially' (xi.5, 186$^{28-31}$).

There is more. Osiander took the noun 'righteousness' and the verb 'to justify' in the sense not only of pardoning sin, but of being made righteous through the indwelling of the Divine essence. Calvin's reply is that, although justification and sanctification are not to be separated, they are not to be confused. Finally, Osiander again by-passes Christ's manhood by saying that the purpose of the preaching of the Gospel, the external Word, is to bring about the reception of the inward Word, the second Person of the Trinity. This, says Calvin, again distracts from Christ the Mediator and the Priest. Certainly the efficacy of Christ's work depends on his being God; but his saving work was done as the Mediator, the Man Christ Jesus.

Justification *consists in the remission of sins.* How is God's rejection turned into acceptance? Not by men ceasing to be sinners, but by God remitting or pardoning their sin. True forgiveness means a change in the relationship between the one who injures and the injured, so that the injury no longer lies between the two. When, therefore, Calvin speaks of forgiveness, he is thinking of the total removal of the injury, of the total sinner being regarded as the totally righteous.

We are brought face to face with the reality and seriousness of the situation in chapter xii: 'To be convinced in real Earnest of our free Justification, our Minds must be lifted up to God's Judgement Seat'.

Man is on trial: 'our discourse is concerned with justice, not of an earthly court but of the heavenly tribunal' (xii.1, 207^{31-32}). The case being tried is whether the man is completely perfect; not perfect by human standards, but so as to satisfy God, 'a perfection such as never has been found in man and never will be' (xii.1, 208^{7-8}). Hence man is guilty and is rightly called to account. It is easy to talk about the 'worthiness of works', says Calvin, in the retirement of scholastic life, but when we come into God's presence all such pleasant chat is at an end. No ridiculous war of words there, but everything deadly serious. 'If we want to enquire fruitfully about true righteousness, then hither, hither, we must turn our minds: How shall we respond to the heavenly Judge when he calls us to account?' (xii.1, 208^{12-15}).

The man on trial knows inescapably that he is guilty. But precisely here is the turning-point. He may surrender himself sullenly and resentfully to despair, or he may accept his guilt and trust still. 'In short, the whole disputation [in chapters xi–xviii] will be insipid and weak unless each of us presents himself as guilty before the heavenly Judge and, anxious to be absolved, freely casts himself down having nothing (*exinanitus*)' (xii.1, 209^{15-17}). So to humble and abase ourselves is to make place, in complete emptiness and poverty, for God's mercy. We notice that Calvin has again dropped into the direct 'preaching' address of the second person singular. It is no longer 'man' that we are to think of as before God's judgement seat, but ourselves.

The Heavenly Judge is the one who is shown in Scripture, 'whose brightness dims the stars, whose power melts mountains, whose wrath shakes the earth, whose wisdom catches the clever in their cunning, in whose purity all things become unclean, whose righteousness not even the Angels can bear, who does not make the guilty innocent, whose vengeance once kindled penetrates even to the depths of hell' (xii.1, 208$^{17-22}$). Let a man do no more than judge himself by the standard of God's Law and he will be humbled into acknowledging his guilt and looking elsewhere for help. And so Calvin turns to Augustine and then more fully to Bernard of Clairvaux to declare where that help is: in the mercies of God through the Mediator. The chapter becomes an exhortation to humility and contrition, much of it in the second person singular: 'When, as so often, thou hearest the word "contrition", think of a wound to the heart that will not let a man felled to the ground get up again. Thy heart must be wounded by such a contrition if it is thy wish to be exalted with the humble, according to God's decree. If not, thou shalt be humbled by the mighty hand of God to thy shame and disgrace' (xii.6, 213$^{33-36}$). This alone is the fit disposition of the guilty sinner before God's judgement seat.

In presenting this doctrine two things must specially be borne in mind. God's glory must emerge undiminished and unimpaired. No Christian will deny that God is righteous. But he must be portrayed as alone righteous and as showing his righteousness precisely in his mercy in justifying. For a man to claim to be righteous is to rob God of that kindness and mercy, inasmuch as to be righteous means that we need, not mercy, but the just reward for our righteousness. It is also to obscure his glory, which becomes, not unique, but only a stronger form of the glory of the man who can glory in his own righteousness. Hence we never give God the glory until we completely abdicate from every claim of our own.

The second consideration is that before God's judgement seat our consciences may have 'placid quiet and serene tranquillity' (xiii.1, 215$^{22-23}$). But how can a conscience enjoy such peace before the all-searching judgement of God? Only by God freely giving righteousness. The corollary to the free gift is faith, having nothing and asking for the free gift. It is the placid quiet and serene tranquillity of faith. Hence, 'To believe is not to waver, to vary, to be carried up and down, to hesitate, to be held in suspense, to stagger, in fact, to despair. It is to hold the mind firm in steadfast certainty and solid security and to have a place where you can set and fix your feet' (xiii.3, 218$^{9-13}$). The promise of mercy, the free gift of righteousness, would have no force if we were justified on account of our righteousness. There remains only faith – as Calvin quaintly puts it, 'the nature of faith is to prick up our ears and shut our eyes' (xiii.4, 219^{21}) – that is, to listen to God's Word and not look at our sins. The foundation of it all is the Cross. The placid quiet and serene tranquillity come only from the sacrifice by which God was reconciled to the world: 'We must seek peace nowhere else but in the terrors of death of Christ our Redeemer' (xiii.4, 219$^{35-36}$).

Calvin continues with a chapter on justification in practice: 'On what is the Beginning of Justification and what its continual Progress'. He sees a fourfold division among men. First, there are those without any knowledge of God and who are sunk in idolatry. Then there are those who have been baptized, but by the impurity of their lives deny the God whom they confess and are Christians in name only. Thirdly, there are the hypocrites, who hide their inward wickedness by outward empty shows. And finally, there are those who are regenerate by the Spirit of God and practise true holiness.

The first are sinners entirely, flesh and nothing but flesh. As we have already seen, the virtues displayed by some good heathens are contaminated by their inward disposition and, measured absolutely, cease to be virtues. They are certainly not meritorious before God. Justification is always free, a gift by God's mercy. So insistent is Calvin on extolling God's mercy that he is half afraid he is protesting too much: 'It keeps occurring to me that I am in danger of injuring God's mercy by labouring so hard to assert it, almost as if it were doubtful or obscure' (xiv.6, 224^6). But then the opposing thought, that we are so ill-disposed that we refuse to give God his due, spurs him on to praise the mercy of God in Christ even more, but now by a string of quotations and references from Scripture, all saying in various ways 'that we are all deadly professed enemies of our God until we are justified and received into his friendship. If the beginning of love is justification, what righteousness of works will precede it?' (xiv.6, 225$^{14-16}$).

In this chapter justification and regeneration are linked in the order of salvation. The Romanist view ran thus: Christ has won our redemption; but to enter into the possession of it we must co-operate with our works. Not so, says Calvin. Certainly we are redeemed by Christ, 'yet, until we are placed in fellowship with him by the calling of the Father, we are heirs of darkness and death and enemies of God' (xiv.6, 225$^{27-29}$).

The second and third groups of men are dealt with more briefly, simply because, in fact, they are in fundamentally no different case from the first. Their polluted consciences betray that they are not yet regenerate, and if not regenerate then also without faith. Hence, they are not yet reconciled and not yet justified. The 'not yet' should be noted. By God's grace they may still repent, believe, and be born again.

Those in the fourth order are the regenerate, those of whom we have heard in chapters iii–x. The question now is whether those who have been justified by faith while they were enemies of God now have good works which will deserve acceptance with God. It has already become clear in those earlier chapters that regeneration does not confer complete holiness and righteousness, but that there always remains imperfection in believers. The imperfection affects all their activities, so that there is no work which, considered in itself, does not deserve reproach. Even if any one work were absolutely pure, what has to be considered is not individual actions, but the whole course of righteousness. If we were to keep nine of the Commandments and break only one, the one transgression is sufficient to make us entirely guilty, as James 2:10 says. On both these accounts, therefore, it is clear that the believer is not justified on account of his own righteousness.

At this point Calvin distinguishes the position of the Reformers from that of what he calls 'the sounder schoolmen'. On the beginning of justification there is no disagreement. The sinner is freely liberated from sin and obtains righteousness by the forgiveness of his sins. The disagreement comes with the interpretation of the word 'justification', in which the schoolmen include also being renewed by the Spirit so as to obey God's Law. Thus the man who is once reconciled to God by faith in Christ can be reckoned righteous for his good works and is accepted by God on account of their merit. The Reformers, on the other hand, say that 'believers have no other righteousness to the end of their lives [than that imputed by God]. For Christ remains the Mediator perpetually, to reconcile the Father to us; and the efficacy of his death is perpetual, namely, washing, satisfaction, expiation, in short, the perfect obedience by which all our iniquities are covered' (xiv.11, 230^{29}–231^5).

This Calvin proceeds to put in philosophical terms, using rather loosely the Aristotelian four causes. If we apply these, he says, we shall find that works cannot be regarded as a cause of our salvation. The efficient cause, according to Scripture, is God's mercy and freely bestowed love. The material cause is Christ and his obedience, by which he won righteousness for us. The formal or instrumental cause must be regarded as faith. These three are stated in John 3:16: 'God so loved the world that he gave his only-begotten Son, that whosoever believeth on him should not perish but have everlasting life.' The final cause is the displaying of God's righteousness and the praise of his goodness. Later Calvin expresses the same points more briefly: 'the effecting of our salvation lies in the love of God the Father; the matter in the obedience of the Son; the instrument in the illumination of the Spirit, that is, faith; the end in the glory of God's so great kindness' (xiv.21, 238^{30-34}).

Christians can certainly gain comfort and strength from the blessings God has given them in the form of good works, but not by claiming those good works as a cause of their justification.

A separate question has now to be asked. Works are not able to justify; but may they not deserve or merit grace in God's eyes? Calvin dislikes the word 'merit', even though it came from the early days of the Church. It is an unnecessary term, not found in Scripture, and has had a pernicious influence on the Church, teaching Christians to think too highly of themselves and too lowly of God's grace. It is true that some fathers used it in a good sense, but, even so, they could have expressed the same truth by a better word. Good works are gifts from God and therefore acceptable to him, and he will reward them. But what is praiseworthy in them is not our activity, but God's grace.

Chapter xviii takes up the subject of rewards. There are many passages in Scripture which affirm that God will recompense every man according to his works. Some of these passages are talking about eternal recompense. But they are not making the works into causes of justification. Rather, they mean that when men have been reconciled to God by faith in the work of the Mediator, and when, therefore, God has begun a good work in them, they must go on to prove that they are the true children of God by walking in obedience to his will.

Faith is not rewarded with righteousness as if it were a virtue: 'The power of justifying which faith possesses does not lie in its value as a work. Our justification stands solely in the mercy of God and the merit of Christ. When faith apprehends this, it is said to justify . . . We say that faith justifies, not because it merits righteousness, but because it is the instrument by which we freely obtain the righteousness of Christ' (xviii.8, 279^{1-10}).

The subject is not yet quite exhausted, however. There remains what Calvin calls the appendix to justification, which is also valuable in bringing out its force. This is Christian liberty, treated in chapter xix. Luther had written a brilliant treatise on it in 1520. Calvin's chapter follows rather a different course.

He looks at the subject from three aspects. The first is freedom from the Law. When it is a question of being justified before God the believer's conscience must rise above the Law 'and forget all the righteousness of the Law'. (This proved too strong meat for Beveridge: 'and think no more of obtaining righteousness by it'; and even Battles in the Library of Christian Classics softens the clause to 'forgetting all Law righteousness'.) In justification there can be no place for the Law. But we should not infer that the Law is superfluous for believers. For there are two quite separate issues here. The one is our acceptance by God. The other is the life of the Christian; and here the Law has the office of warning, exhorting, and stimulating to holiness and innocence.

The second aspect is the spirit in which the believer views the Law. He obeys the Law, not by forced necessity, as a slave obeys a tyrannical master, but spontaneously and willingly because it expresses the will of his heavenly Father. This too is a matter of freedom, freedom from fear of the Law and the consequences of not obeying. Yet although Calvin calls this obedience spontaneous and willing he is aware that there is a hard fight as well: 'For although they love God with their minds and with a sincere affection of their hearts, they still have part of their hearts and souls possessed by the desires of the "flesh" . . . They wish, they aspire, they strive; but nothing is perfect as it should be' (xix.4, 285$^{4-11}$). The spontaneity lies in the spirit in which they seek to obey the Law.

The third aspect concerns things which are neither good nor bad in themselves, the so-called 'things indifferent' – in Greek, the *adiaphora*. Liberty in this case means that they may be used or not. Believers must not have a bad conscience about them; nor may other persons (not even the Church, without the command of Scripture) impose binding regulations on them. We are talking about such matters as keeping certain days holy, or eating flesh, or fasting. All this soon becomes a dreadful labyrinth from which it is hard to escape: 'If anyone doubts whether it is right for him to use linen for table-cloths, underclothes, handkerchiefs, table napkins, he will afterwards not feel safe with hemp, and at last will have scruples about using the coarsest of cloth, for he will be worrying whether perhaps he could not dine without a table napkin or even do without a handkerchief. If he worries about drinking a better vintage of wine he will go on to be unable to drink some rot-gut with a quiet conscience, and in the end will not dare to touch water that is sweeter and cleaner than the rest' (xix.7, 287^{3-12}). So we may use God's good gifts with a clear conscience – and give him thanks. But this must not be taken as an excuse for pleasing ourselves or giving way to licence or extravagance. It is as wrong to insist on eating meat on Fridays because we are free to do so, as it is to insist that no meat be eaten on Fridays. Sufficient to be aware that we have the freedom even if we do not use it. For liberty must always be used with thought of others and their consciences, and giving them offence.

Offences are of two sorts, offences given and offences taken. We are responsible for the former; the latter are beyond our control. Calvin calls the former 'the offence of the weak'; that is, of those who, because they do not fully understand or have not yet fully achieved liberty, have consciences that are easily hurt. Such people we must respect, and take pains not to give offence to them (although, at the same time, they ought to be taught and led out of their weakness into real Christian liberty). But as for the others, who take offence, theirs is 'the offence of the Pharisees' (who were continually taking the actions and sayings of Jesus hypercritically and unfairly). To them there must be no yielding.

Some Anabaptists applied their Christian liberty to their relationship with the State, as if they were free from all State control. It is to this problem that Calvin finally turns, anticipating what he was going to write in Book IV. There is a twofold government for the believer, a spiritual and a temporal, 'the spiritual kingdom' and 'the political kingdom'. It is necessary to consider them as being separate, because there are, so to say, two worlds within the believer, with different kings and with separate laws. So far there is little difficulty. But it seems as if conscience is involved in both respects, conscience as a believer in regard to God's Laws and conscience as a citizen in regard to civil laws. Hence it would appear that Christian liberty is involved in each. Not so, says Calvin. Conscience, strictly speaking, is directed towards God, not to man. Hence conscience in respect of civil government is still conscience towards God. This means that Christians are not free from obedience to the State, but that their obedience is a matter of their liberty towards God.

4 ON PRAYER

A hasty reading might conclude that the subjects in Book III, chapters xx–xxv were a mixed bag thrown in here because they had to go somewhere. But if we pay careful attention to the 'stage-directions' we shall see that there is good reason for the ordering.

We might even say that the *Institutio* reaches its climax here. Certainly Calvin suggests that he was drawing together in chapter xx all that he had said previously: 'On Prayer, which is the chief Exercise of Faith and by which we daily receive God's Benefits'. If the title puts this chapter in its place in the discussion on faith (i.e., all of Book III), the opening sentence opens a wider view: 'From those things which have been discussed up to now . . . ' (296[33]). And from what follows it is plain that we must cast our minds back to the first chapter of Book I, for he now repeats what he had said there. Man is empty of all good things; he lacks everything that will assist in his salvation. Therefore, he must go outside himself and obtain from elsewhere what he lacks. Afterwards, Calvin goes on, it was explained that God revealed himself in Christ, offering in him happiness in place of misery, riches for our poverty, and, therefore, that our faith must look wholly to Christ and all our hope must be set in him. (This was the subject of Book II.) This self-revelation of God in Christ is 'a secret and hidden philosophy', which cannot be learned by logical inference, but only by God's enlightening us. Faith is born from hearing the Gospel, and 'by faith our hearts are formed to call upon the name of God' (xx.1, 297[20–22]). But in speaking of faith we are also speaking of the Holy Spirit, who in Romans 8:16 is called 'the Spirit of adoption' and by whom we cry 'Abba, Father!' Because this last point has been touched on only lightly, he says, it must now be treated more fully.

His view of prayer is simple. Fundamentally, it is asking God for what we lack. He conceives of a heavenly treasure-house of God, full of all good things. By means of prayer we reach those riches: 'For there is a certain communication of men with God by which, when they enter into the heavenly sanctuary, they appeal before him concerning his promises' (xx.2, 297[31–32]). But then he alters the image to that of the treasure found in the field: 'by prayer we dig up the treasures which our faith has seen set out by the Gospel of the Lord' (xx.2, 297[36]–298[1]). 'Appealing to God' and 'digging up the treasure' are poetic ways of saying that we ask God for what he has promised.

Yet prayer is not simply a seeking of God's blessings. Rather, it is a calling for his presence, for the presence of his Providence caring for us, of his power upholding us and of his goodness receiving us, who are laden with sin, into his favour: 'in short, in which we call for himself wholly, that he may show himself to us as present with us' (xx.2, 298$^{8-9}$).

The corollary of seeking God and his blessings is laying before him our troubles and needs. If we do this, we shall have rest and tranquillity in our consciences. But does not God know our needs without being told? Certainly, but this is not so much for God's sake as for our own. God has the right of having all good things referred to him and not treated as if they belonged to man. Anyone who believes this will ask God to supply them to him. Hence prayer testifies to the reality and strength of the belief. It is true that God gives without being asked. But if we continually go to him in prayer 'our heart is inflamed with an earnest and burning desire to seek, love, and worship him' (xx.3, 298^{37}–299^{2}). Again, in going to God we know that no thought which we are ashamed for him to see should enter our mind. And, lastly, continual praying will beget praise and thanksgiving. For all these reasons prayer is for our sake rather than God's.

When Calvin proceeds to set out four 'laws of right praying', he is treading a well-trodden path. But we must not take these as regulations for those who would learn that strange practice called 'the art of prayer', but must refer them to the context of the *Institutio*.

The first 'law' concerns the control of thoughts. Everything foreign to our purpose in the prayer must be driven out; we must, in a sense, rise above ourselves and not be constricted to the narrow limits of our inward emptiness. But more than this, our thoughts and wishes must not be allowed a free rein. We must ask nothing but what God allows us. We must ask according to his will and under the guidance of his Spirit. This does not mean that we are to leave all the praying to the Spirit. On the contrary, we must strive to pray.

The second 'law' is that we must in prayer feel our own poverty and so be moved to pray with an earnest, even burning, desire. There can be nothing perfunctory about prayer. Nor should our requests be blurted out without thought. It is a matter of hungering and thirsting for what we ask. The objection that we do not at all times have the same urgent need is invalid. Even if it is partly true in earthly matters, we have still to remember that all that we already possess is God's gift; we must pray for its continuance. In regard to spiritual things, however, there is always need for such hungering and thirsting. What is more, because we are sinners, there can be no praying without repentance and a spirit of penitence: 'genuine prayer demands repentance' (xx.7, 304²⁶⁻²⁷). If anyone is set deliberately against God, he cannot expect to be heard. Therefore, he must come as a penitent, even as a beggar, possessing nothing.

The third 'law' continues this thought. In prayer we must abdicate all idea of our own glory, all opinion of our own worth, all trust in ourselves. The glory must be given to God completely and wholly. This is what we might call the 'law' of justification by faith alone. Therefore, the basis for right prayer and the proper preparation for prayer is intercession for pardon and a humble and open confession of guilt. Hence prayer must be grounded on God's free mercy. Yet sometimes in Scripture the saints appeal to their own righteousness. This does not, however, mean that they were trusting in their righteousness, so that God had to repay them by granting their requests. Nor is prayer itself a meritorious work. The saints only showed that they were conscious of being God's children and as such might call on him as their Father.

The fourth 'law' is the assurance of obtaining what is asked for because God is faithful to his promises. Such assurance goes hand in hand with penitence. It is not an assurance devoid of all anxiety and fear. The two, confidence, or faith, and anxiety, are both present. The believer is in prayer both penitent and believing, both anxious and confident.

These four 'laws' are not intended to be so strictly enforced as if God would reject any prayer not prayed according to this standard. If God were extreme to mark what is done amiss, no prayer would ever be heard by him. In this as in all the other activities of the believer God is an indulgent Father, accepting even the most imperfect attempts of his children. The central thing is that all prayer should be from faith in Christ, prayed in unison with Christ who is himself our Advocate and Mediator with God. We cannot come to God directly, but only by the mediation of the crucified Christ. He intercedes for us in the sense that he presents his crucified body before the Father: 'We do not imagine that he throws himself on his knees before the Father, praying for us as a suppliant. But with the Apostle we understand that he so appeared before the face of God that the power of his death avails as an intercession for us for ever – and yet in such a way that, having entered the heavenly sanctuary, he alone brings to God, until the consummation of the ages, the wishes of his people dwelling in the outer courts' (xx.20, 325²⁶⁻³²).

This is the priestly office of Christ. As under the old Covenant the High Priest, with the names of the twelve tribes on his shoulders, entered into the sanctuary with the blood of sacrifice for the sins of the people, so Christ has entered into the presence of the Father with his own blood: 'that shadowy ceremony of the Law taught us that we are all far from God's face and that therefore we need a Mediator to appear in our name and bear us on his shoulders and keep us bound on his breast so that we might be heard in his person. And our prayers must be cleansed by the sprinkling of blood, for otherwise they would never, as we said, be free from uncleanness' (xx.18, 323$^{9-14}$). It is, then, not simply a matter of praying *through* Christ, but rather *with* Christ, of our prayers being united with his intercession for us. Thus Christ becomes the precentor who leads the prayers of his people. There can be no question of Christ's intercession removing the need for the prayers of believers, but rather of all their prayers depending on the intercession of their High Priest and being heard as one with his prayer. This concept will be further strengthened when we hear in Book IV that the Church consists of Christ and his people.

The fact that prayer is to be viewed as the exercise of faith and therefore as inescapably united with Christ alone means that Calvin, with the Reformers in general, was in conflict with the prevailing Romanist belief in the mediatorial intercession of saints. By confining Christ's mediatorial office to redemption and transferring the succeeding mediatorial intercession to believers, the 'sophists' were, he says, robbing Christ of a part of his honour. It is true that believers must pray for one another; but only Christ is the eternal Mediator, whether in dying for sin or in presenting his death to God in abiding intercession for his people.

As for imploring the aid of saints who are dead; if they do pray for the living, it is only through Christ. But there is nothing in Scripture about such prayers by departed saints. In every way it is a pernicious practice: it makes Christ insufficient as an intercessor or too strict to intercede for sinners; it dishonours him by removing or diminishing his mediatorial office; it empties the Cross and all that Christ did of its efficacy; it even destroys the Fatherhood of God, for God is not our Father unless Christ is our Brother.

But, he says, they go even further. Departed saints are given their own particular sphere of influence and so have little by little been changed from *divus* (saint) into *deus* (God). They are now become guardian gods to whom men call for help.

It is no doubt true that departed saints have no less care for God's kingdom and the salvation of believers than they had when they were on earth. And it may be granted that they pray for the living in this way. But this does not give us warrant for calling on them. All this is only conjecture; we have little information about their state. The scriptural evidence that is brought forward in support of the practice will not stand up to examination. Prayer is an exercise of faith, and faith is grounded in the Scriptures: 'faith, the mother of praying, is founded on the Word. As soon as it is turned aside from the Word, prayer is necessarily adulterated. But it has already been demonstrated that if we consult the whole of Scripture, this honour [of being called upon] is claimed for God alone' (xx.27, 333[38]–334[3]).

Calvin returns to his positive teaching. Prayer and thanksgiving belong together, so that without gratitude prayer is feeble and lacklustre. It is obvious that there should be giving of thanks when prayers have been clearly answered; but the thanksgiving should precede the answers and should be an integral part of prayer. The one praying prays from his faith, and if from his faith then with trust in God's promises that he will hear the prayer and that whoever asks will receive. Even when the believer is in trouble and heaviness the thanksgiving is present, even if latent. More, thanksgiving is not a simple 'thank you', but a whole attitude of ascribing all to God's kindness and hence of loving the Giver: 'God's benefits not only claim the praise of the tongue but also win naturally our love . . . Praises which do not flow from this sweetness of love will never praise God' (xx.28, 337[9–15]).

Paul tells us to pray without ceasing, to be persistent in praying. This is true for public prayers as well as for private. Certainly, church services do not go on all the time but are held at set times for the convenience of the people. But sometimes a Church may be moved to have more frequent prayers than usual.

Christ forbade his disciples to use long prayers (Matt 6:7), but this was not against frequency or actual length or the fervency of prayers, but against, so to say, 'nagging' God or simply the long-windedness which may be a sign of insincerity. Again, his condemnation of praying in front of other people (Matt 6:6) means only that we should find a quiet place which will be conducive to our concentrating in mind and heart, 'for he promises that the God whose temples our bodies ought to be will be close to the feelings of our minds' (xx.29, 339[20–21]).

Both private and public prayer are necessary for believers. He that neglects the one will neglect the other also. The Temple was called 'the house of prayer' because 'the chief part of his worship . . . is the office of praying' (xx.29, 340[7–8]). Modern churches are places for common prayer and it is the duty of believers to join in the meetings there. This does not mean, however, that God in-habits that particular building in a special way or that they have a 'secret holiness' which is imparted to the prayers made in them. According to Paul, the temples of God are believers.

Calvin has already said that prayers must come from the heart. This is also true of public prayers and congregational singing. If, however, both the words and the singing do come from the heart they are commendable, for our tongues were created for the very purpose of praising God. There is a word of caution here. Singing in church is a very ancient custom; the New Testament speaks of the Apostles singing praises. But it was not a universal custom in the early Church. According to Augustine's *Confessions* (ix.7), in Milan it began only under Ambrose. It cannot, therefore, be regarded as one of the absolute necessities. Yet it is a powerful instrument in stirring up and exalting men's spirits. But we have to beware lest we pay more attention to the music than to the words.

Public prayers must be in the language that the congregation under-stands, for they are for the upbuilding of all in the congregation. The Romanists are wrong to have services in Latin in ordinary churches.

In paragraphs 34–48 Calvin expounds the Lord's Prayer as 'a form in which, as if tabulated, [Christ] set before us all that it is right to desire from him, all that is profitable for us, all that it is necessary to ask' (xx.34, 344^{12-14}). The fact that there are many other prayers in the New Testament shows that Christ did not mean that believers should use no other form of prayer, but that this should be regulatory of all prayers.

Later, Calvin gives simple and sometimes practical advice on praying. The believer should observe set hours of prayer – when he gets up in the morning, before he starts work, before and after meals, and when he goes to bed at night. He does not intend them as rigid rules, binding on consciences, but only as a discipline to help the weakness that everyone has in praying. Nor have we to confine ourselves to such hours. There will be times when we are pressed by some circumstance or other to turn to God.

We must not order God about in our prayers, treating him as if he were at our beck and call, and telling him when and where and how we want this or that to be done. Every request must be 'according to thy will'. It is God, not the believer, who is the Lord. Again, God may not at once give any apparent answer to prayer. This will prove to be a test of the believer's faith. Let him keep on asking, and the very delay in answering will be a spur to his faith. Besides, it may be that there was no delay and that the prayer was answered either negatively or in a different form from what was expected. But answer God will: 'Although all things may fail, God will never desert us, never disappoint the expectation and patience of his people' (xx.52, 368[3–5]). Therefore, persevere in prayer!

5 ETERNAL ELECTION

We are brought in chapters xxi–xxiv to the doctrine of election: 'On the Eternal Election by which God predestines Some to Salvation, Others to Destruction'. Because this doctrine has been the subject of many and bitter controversies, dividing otherwise like-minded Christians (as among Evangelicals in eighteenth-century England), and because Calvin has been regarded by the less well-informed as almost exclusively a teacher of predestination, we must pay particular heed to the context of these chapters.

A very brief word about the history of the doctrine before Calvin will set the context.[4] It was Augustine who, in opposition to the teaching of Pelagius, developed the doctrine in the form which was to be taken as definitive up to the twentieth century. After him theologians were, in regard to this doctrine, either Augustinian, semi-Augustinian, or anti-Augustinian. There was no stepping outside the magic circle that he had drawn round predestination. During the Middle Ages there was a renewed controversy in the ninth century. Augustinian theologians like Aquinas naturally followed Augustine; but later, in the fourteenth and fifteenth centuries, the trend, despite strong Augustinians like Bradwardine, was towards semi-Pelagianism rather than semi-Augustinianism. This trend continued in the sixteenth century, with works like Erasmus's *On the Freedom of the Will*, to which Luther had replied with *On the Bondage of the Will*.[5] Calvin himself stood firmly within the Augustinian tradition; indeed, J. B. Mozley said that he could find no essential difference between the doctrines of Augustine, Aquinas and Calvin.[6]

The setting of this doctrine in the *Institutio* was changed for the final edition. In the 1539–50 recensions it was treated as a part of the doctrine of Providence. This was in line with Aquinas. In 1559, however, we find it placed in Book III between the chapters on prayer and the final resurrection. Broadly speaking we should expect chapters xxi–xxiv to be somehow illustrative of the title of the Book (*On the Way we Receive the Grace of Christ and what Fruits come to us from it* [i.e., the grace] *and what Effects follow*).

How do these chapters explain the way in which we receive the grace of Christ? Throughout the Book the cause of salvation has been put as God's free mercy, from the giving of Christ as Mediator to the calling of salvation in Christ alone in the Gospel.

It is here that the justification for the position of the doctrine of election exists, as the opening sentence of chapter xxi shows: 'But now, because the Covenant of life is not preached equally to all, and among those to whom it is preached it does not equally or perpetually find the same place, in this diversity the wonderful height of the Divine judgement shows itself' (xxi.1, 368[33–36]). Why do some believe and some not believe when the same Gospel is preached to the same sort of people? Because God calls some and rejects others. Predestination for Calvin, as for Augustine before him, was a pastoral or evangelistic problem.

We should not, he goes on, regard the doctrine as dark and gloomy and frightening, but as offering sweet fruit, because it teaches us that salvation is by God's free mercy. It is obvious that, if God has made a choice, we are accepted by him before there could be any question of inherent goodness or good works or merits. Election buttresses the doctrine of justification by faith alone. It is the foundation of our salvation.

Nevertheless, a serious warning is given against curiosity and wandering off into forbidden bypaths. Anyone who bursts rashly and recklessly into 'the inmost shrine of the Divine wisdom' (xxi.1, 370[21]) will end up without his curiosity being satisfied, and find himself lost in a labyrinth from which he cannot escape. God's wisdom is to be adored, not snatched at. God has declared in his Word the secrets of his will so far as concerns us and is useful to us. To seek any knowledge of predestination apart from what is declared in God's Word is foolishness, a trying to see in total darkness.

A warning is needed also for those who are frightened of the doctrine. Here again, keep to the Word: 'Scripture is the school of the Holy Spirit. In it nothing is omitted that is necessary and useful to know, nothing is taught that is not beneficial to know' (xxi.3, 372[1–3]). While the Lord speaks, listen! When he stops speaking, stop enquiring! If we were deterred by objections and slanders we should never teach anything at all.

We come to the doctrine itself. The principle, which all believers should hold, is that 'God adopts some to the hope of life and adjudges others to eternal death' (xxi.5, 373[33–34]). The usual objection here is that God did not predestine, but foreknew. This had been Augustine's original position. In reply Calvin first defines the two concepts: 'When we ascribe foreknowledge to God we mean that everything always has been and perpetually will remain under his eyes, so that in his knowing there is nothing future or past but all things are present . . . Predestination, however, we call God's eternal decree by which he holds determined with himself what he wishes to become of each man. For not all are created in the same condition. For some eternal life is preordained, for others eternal condemnation' (xxi.5, 374[4-15]).

To show that Scripture teaches predestination and not merely foreknowledge, Calvin shows that it is clear from the Old Testament that Israel was chosen by God and that this involved the segregation of the one race from all the other nations who had not been chosen. Israel was chosen, not for any inherent quality, nor for its righteousness, but solely by God's good pleasure. Within Israel, however, a choice was made. Isaac was chosen and not Ishmael, Jacob and not Esau.

In all this, but especially in the choice of individuals, it is the freedom of God's grace and kindness that is especially illustrated. Yet even individual election is not the heart of the matter: 'for election to be efficacious and truly firm we must ascend to the Head, in whom the heavenly Father collects together his elect and joins them to himself by an unbreakable bond' (xxi.7, 377[26-29]). Christ is the pattern of all election. If we wish to understand it, we must look at his election. This will be developed further in Calvin's next chapter. For the present he concentrates on individual Israelites. God showed his generous favour by adopting the offspring of Abraham in general, and yet this was denied to some among them. It is not like that with Christ, the offspring of Abraham. Not all who belong to Abraham's family by birth are elected to life, but 'in the members of Christ a far superior power of grace is conspicuous in that, ingrafted in their Head, they are never cut off from their salvation' (xxi.7, 377[30-32]).

The final part of chapter xxi shows clearly that Calvin intends to treat this doctrine in terms of justification, which is by God's free mercy and to which men are called by the preaching of the Gospel. 'The Lord designates [who are] his elect by calling and justification' and he designates those who are rejected 'by excluding them either from a knowledge of his name or from the sanctifying of his Spirit' (xxi.7, 379[7-9]). Some hear the Gospel, believe and are justified; others either never have the opportunity of hearing it or do not effectively accept and believe it.

That Calvin's doctrine is not to be interpreted as a form of philosophical determinism is shown by the title of the next chapter: 'Confirmation of this Doctrine by Testimonies from Scripture'. He considered that he was repeating only what was plainly taught in the Bible and given a classic form by Augustine (whose anti-Pelagian works he quotes very freely).

He now comes to the election of Christ. Before Jesus had done anything meritorious he was chosen in the womb to become 'the Head of the Angels, the only-begotten Son of God, the image and glory of the Father, light, righteousness, the salvation of the world' (xxii.1, 380$^{19-21}$). As Augustine said, Christ is the clearest image of free election. He was not made the Son on account of his righteousness but was freely given this honour, so that he might make others partakers of his gifts. Hence if we refuse God's right to choose and reject we have also to reject Christ as God's 'chosen one' (Matt 12:18).

The scriptural starting-point is Ephesians 1:4–6: 'he chose us in Christ before the foundation of the world, that we should be holy and blameless before him in love, having predestinated us to the adoption of children by Jesus Christ to himself, according to the good pleasure of his will, to the praise of the glory of his grace, wherein he has made us accepted in the Beloved'. This, Calvin says, is equivalent to saying 'because the heavenly Father found nothing worthy of his choice in the whole family of Adam, he turned his eyes to his Christ, that he might choose as members of [Christ's] body those whom he would take into the community of life' (xxii.1, 381$^{2-5}$). But he expounds the passage in more detail. Those who are *chosen* means believers. That they were chosen *before the creation of the world* removes all possibility of their being chosen for their worthiness, since they did not yet even exist. They are chosen *in him*, that is, in Christ, so that the choice lies outside each individual and within this other; moreover, it implies a segregation among men, in that we see that not all are members of Christ. That they are chosen *in order that they might be holy* is a clear if tacit denial of a mere foreknowledge of their holiness; holiness is the effect of election. And that the election was *according to the good pleasure of his will* shows the higher cause of the choice in that it was because God so predestined, 'because God chooses whom he will' (xxii.2, 382^2).

After bringing forward many other passages from Scripture, Calvin turns to the teaching of Christ himself in a series of sayings recorded in the Fourth Gospel. These are highly important in

Calvin's doctrine and we must quote some of them. 'All that the Father gives me will come to me' (6:37); 'that I should lose nothing of all that he has given me' (6:39); 'everyone who has heard and learned from the Father comes to me' (6:45); 'I have manifested thy name to the men whom thou gavest me out of the world; thine they were, and thou gavest them to me' (17:6); 'I have kept in thy name those whom thou hast given me' (17:12). All these verses say very clearly that some men belonged to God the Father who gave them to the incarnate Son. The belonging was not as creatures but only by God's grace: 'the whole world [of men] does not belong to its Creator; but grace snatches from God's curse and wrath and from eternal death a few who would otherwise have perished' (xxii.7, 387²⁴⁻²⁶). Of the eternal Son, the second Person of the Trinity, it must be said that he with the Father and the Holy Spirit is the God who makes the choice. For in John 13:18 Christ says 'I know whom I have chosen'. Thus 'Christ makes himself the author of election' (xxii.7, 387³⁶⁻³⁷).

It had been said earlier in the Book that by the preaching of the Gospel all are called to repentance and faith, but that the Spirit of repentance and faith is not given to all. We hear in Acts 16:6–7, for example, that Paul was forbidden by the Spirit to preach in Asia and Bithynia. The inference is that the Spirit had the freedom to choose to whom the Gospel should be preached. Again, even where it is preached, the mere words will not convert the hearers into God's children, but only their faith, the work of the Spirit. In the parable of the sower (Matt 13:3ff.) some seed fell by the wayside, some on stony ground, some among thorns; for 'not all have been endowed with eyes and ears so as to understand' (xxii.10, 391³⁷).

As for the rejected, they are not rejected by God because of their works. In the case of Jacob and Esau neither good nor bad had been done by either, but according to Romans 9:13, before they were born 'Jacob I loved and Esau I hated'. Is God therefore unjust? Not at all. Paul's reply is not what we should expect, that God hated Esau for his wickedness, but 'that the rejected are raised up in order that the glory of God may be brought to light through them' (xxii.11, 393²⁴⁻²⁵). We are to seek no reason for rejection, any more than for acceptance, outside God's will.

This last point may be amplified from passages in the next chapter – a chapter we may pass over as consisting of a 'Refutation of the Calumnies with which this Doctrine has always unjustly been loaded'. Nevertheless, it is well worth the reading to see how Calvin replies to the sort of objections which this doctrine commonly encounters. First, the objection that it would be unfair for God to be angry with men *before* they had offended. No, says Calvin, it is enough to say that this was God's will. To ask why he so willed is to try to go beyond and behind God, which is impossible. There is nothing above God's will, 'the supreme rule of righteousness, so that whatever he wills is to be held righteous simply because he wills it' (xxiii.2, 396$^{3-4}$). He denies that this is an assertion of *potentia absoluta*, a doctrine he regards as profane and detestable. God is not lawless. We are saying only that God does not have to account for his actions to us and that we are not fit judges to pronounce on God's will. Moreover, God's will must not be considered in abstraction but in relation to what we know him to be like from Scripture. There he declares that he loves righteousness and hates iniquity. If this is so, how can he act unjustly?

We take up again at the end of chapter xxiii the question of the place of preaching in predestination. It is objected that if God chooses some and rejects others even before the earth was made there is no point in preaching, since God's will cannot be changed. But Paul's doctrine of predestination did not prevent him preaching and also writing exhortations to holiness. This is the theme also of chapter xxiv: 'Election is confirmed by God's Calling; but the Rejected procure for themselves the just Destruction to which they were destined'. God's call is through the Gospel and is put into effect when the Gospel is declared in preaching. On the other hand, the same preaching of the Gospel has the effect of blinding and hardening the ungodly. The call of God in preaching is thus the revealing of his election. Calvin calls it *testificatio*, a Ciceronian word meaning a giving evidence or showing proof of something. In God's effectual calling of a man he is giving proof that this person has been chosen in Christ before the foundation of the world. Conversely, those whom God has chosen do not enter into possession of their election and adoption as children until they are called. When they are called, they receive the Spirit, who is the Spirit of adoption. The calling is a stage on the path of election to eternal life: 'Although the preaching of the Gospel flows out of the spring of election, yet because it is also common to the rejected, it would not in itself be a firm proof of election. But God teaches his elect efficaciously so that he may lead them to faith' (xxiv.1, 410$^{25-28}$). The very calling is of God's free mercy. Nor should it be overlooked that in the election of man there is involved a certain self-determination of God, a self-determination to the Fatherhood of sons:

'whom God elects he designates as his children, and destines himself to be their Father. Moreover, by calling he adopts them into his own family and unites himself with them so that they may be one' (xxiv.1, 411$^{20-22}$).

Calling is a matter of God's choice. It does not consist only in the message of the Gospel but also in the enlightening of mind and heart by the Holy Spirit. Hence it is not merely an outward calling in words but an inward call by the Spirit, as we heard in III.i. Since the Spirit works freely, the inward calling is by the free kindness of God.

It is not that in preaching man is only offered a choice of believing or not believing. He is given faith itself; that is, faith in Christ as his Redeemer. Election does not depend on faith, but it is confirmed inwardly by faith. God's secret and hidden counsel is brought to light, 'so that what had been unknown is confirmed and as it were attested with a seal' (xxiv.3, 413$^{18-19}$). Hence assurance of one's election lies in faith in the Gospel, in which God's will is opened up to us, and not 'in trying to penetrate into God's eternal ordination [which] will engulf us in a profound abyss' (xxiv.3, 413$^{22-23}$).

It is the work of Satan to make a believer doubt and wonder if he is elect and so try 'to burst into the hidden chambers of the Divine wisdom and understand what has been determined about himself at God's judgement seat . . . For then he will be casting himself down to be swallowed up in the depths of an infinite chasm; he will be entangling himself in numberless inextricable snares; he will be burying himself in an abyss of blind darkness' (xxiv.4, 414$^{14-19}$). Hence the mere consideration of predestination is like sailing perilous seas. We may all too easily make shipwreck by steering a wrong course. But it will be a safe and peaceful voyage, even a happy one, if we keep to what we are taught in God's Word.

To be taught in God's Word entails first and foremost fixing our eyes on Christ, the fountain of life, the author of salvation. To be chosen by God is to be adopted as God's children, so as to obtain salvation and eternal life by the grace of Christ. We are not elected in ourselves but in Christ. It is only in Christ that God can love us. Therefore, assurance of our salvation is certainly not to be grounded on anything in ourselves, not even in God the Father considered apart from Christ: 'We have a sufficiently clear and firm testimony that we are written in the book of life if we are united with Christ' (xxiv.5, 416$^{7-9}$). And we are united with Christ when we believe through the preaching of the Gospel.

Again, and in accord with faith in Christ being the foundation of assurance of election, the very assurance is a spur to calling upon God. A shallow view of election would imagine that such assurance would render prayer unnecessary. On the contrary, it animates the believer to pray. It would be preposterous to pray in doubt of our election. There can be no 'O Lord! hear me if I am elect'. This is still trying to go straight to a knowledge of election apart from Christ. As we saw in the last chapter, our prayers can only be through and in Christ, in union with the intercession of the Christ in whom we are chosen. We must be satisfied with God's promises in Christ.

A further confirmation is to be found in Jesus' teaching in John 10. He is the Shepherd of the sheep, who not only receives those whom the Father brings to him but also keeps them safe, so that 'none can pluck them out of my hand'. Here we are no longer in the past, 'before the creation of the world', or in the present with God's calling; but in the future, for which this is a promise. Of course, we must not presume on this and fall into a facile 'once saved, always saved' frame of mind, no longer humble and fearful, neglecting prayer for perseverance. The believer's perseverance depends on Christ's power, not his own. Nevertheless, we may rely on Christ's promise that when he makes us his own we are safe in his keeping.

This, however, seems against the facts. It is a common thing to see people who apparently belong to Christ fall away from him. The answer is, says Calvin, that they were never really Christians. This reinforces our need to trust Christ's promise and to walk humbly. The saying of Jesus, 'Many are called, but few are chosen' (Matt 22:14), is commonly misunderstood. Properly it refers to two kinds of calling, a general call in which all are called through the preaching of the Gospel, and a special call when the Spirit illuminates the mind. This latter is given mostly only to the elect. Sometimes the rejected may be enlightened by the Spirit for a time, after which he leaves them and they fall into still deeper darkness.

God's calling of his elect does not occur at birth but at some time in their lives when he thinks fit. Until they are called, there is nothing to differentiate the elect from the rejected; they wander outside the saving knowledge of God. Yet all the time God holds them, so to say, on a long rein and keeps them from 'rushing over the final precipice of death' (xxiv.10, 421^{22-23}). Calvin here disagrees with Bucer, who saw this restraint as a 'seed of election' which was in the elect from birth and inclined them to *pietas*.[7] Ephesians 2:3 is clear, says Calvin, that before calling the elect were 'by nature children of wrath, like the others'. The protection that God gives the elect before their calling goes no further than keeping them 'from falling headlong into irreconcilable blasphemy' (xxiv.11, 423$^{17-18}$). A door is kept unlocked for calling, faith, justification and regeneration in God's good time.

Paragraphs 12 to the end are concerned with rejection. To fulfil his plan of rejection God works in two ways. Sometimes, as we have seen, he deprives people of any opportunity of hearing the Gospel. For example, it was some two thousand years from the calling of Abraham until the Gentiles were permitted to hear the promise as addressed to them. The second way is that God blinds some of those who hear the Gospel. If, Calvin says, the same sermon is preached to one hundred people, only twenty will embrace it in faith, while the rest will reject it with varying degrees of determination.

This is the question with which Calvin began the discussion of predestination in chapter xxi. He repeats what he had said then: 'Why then does God bestow grace on these but passes over those?' Answer: because he has ordained these to life while those are 'vessels of wrath unto contumely' (Rom 9:21). There are many examples in Scripture of God's hardening men's hearts, notably Pharaoh (Exod 4:21). This is not merely an accidental effect of God's Word but is God's intention in sending the Word: 'Behold! he directs his voice to them, but it is in order to harden them the more: he kindles a light, but it is in order to make them more blind' (xxiv.13, 425$^{16-17}$). Christ said that he taught in parables 'in order that seeing, they might see and not perceive, and hearing they may hear and not understand' (Matt 13:13), whereas to the disciples 'it was given to know the mysteries of the kingdom of heaven'. Yet, adds Calvin, it was still their own fault for not understanding. Even in parables they were given enough light to convict their consciences of ungodliness; but they rejected the light.

Why does God act in this way? Ultimately because the rejected 'are raised up by God's inscrutable judgement to illustrate his glory by their condemnation' (xxiv.14, 426$^{4-5}$). Some say that God is thereby made into a monster cruelly playing with men according to a *potentia inordinata*. Not so. 'The rejected suffer nothing but what accords with the most righteous judgement of God. We do not understand the reason for it; but let us not refuse to have some ignorance when the wisdom of God rises to its full sublimity' (xxiv.14, 426^{35}–427^2). And his final word is to quote Romans 9:20: 'Who are you, O man, to contend with God?'

6 THE FINAL RESURRECTION

We reach the culmination of the *Institutio*. In chapter xxv of Book III Calvin weaves together the substance of the work into its conclusion. Not only the subjects but also particular phrases direct us back to this or that doctrine or line of thought. The first sentence carries us through Books II and III: 'Christ, the Sun of righteousness, having overcome death, shines through the Gospel and illuminates us with life, so that by believing we are said to pass from death to life and are no longer wanderers and foreigners but citizens with the saints and the household of God . . . so that nothing is wanting to our full happiness' (xxv.1, 432$^{10-16}$). Yet, Calvin goes on, we must remember what was said in Book III, chapter ii on the nature of hope, so that we may not be crushed when we compare our present afflictions with such blessings. We must remember that 'whatever has previously been explained about our salvation demands minds raised up to heaven, so that we may love the Christ we have not seen and believing in him may rejoice with unspeakable and glorious joy until we attain the end of our faith' (xxv.1, 432^{31}–433^{3}). We must not allow any earthly thing to deflect our gaze from Christ. Only the man who exercises himself continually in 'the meditation of the blessed resurrection' (echoes of chapter ix of Book III) has really profited from hearing the Gospel.

Philosophers have argued about the *summum bonum*, the supreme good. None of them, with the exception of Plato, realized that it consisted in union with God (and even Plato had not the remotest notion what this union was, because he had never learned anything about the bond of the union – that is, Christ as Mediator, the work of the Spirit, and faith). Believers, however, know this unique and perfect felicity even in this world. Yet they know it in such a way that they continually desire to know it more and more until they shall be satisfied with the fruition of it in the world to come.

But it is not only believers, out of all creation, that have this hope. The whole of creation shares this expectation. By his fall Adam ruptured the sound order of nature, leaving it in bondage to mortality and corruption. Nevertheless, all things, even the insensible, have a natural appetite for what they had once been and from which they are fallen. 'The whole creation groaneth and travaileth in pain together until now, awaiting . . . ' (Rom 8:22). Believers should be ashamed if they have not the same longing for redemption.

The importance of the resurrection is so great that, if the dead did not rise, the whole of the Gospel would be empty and false (1 Cor 15:14) – not merely a part of it, but 'the whole sum of it, which embraces both adoption and the effect of our salvation' (xxv.3, 434$^{25-26}$). This could perhaps have been dealt with earlier, but 'I have deferred until this place what ought to be said about it, so that readers may learn that when they receive Christ, the author of perfect salvation, they should ascend even higher and know him clothed in heavenly immortality and glory, in order that the whole body may be conformed to the Head' (xxv.3, 434$^{27-32}$). The resurrection of believers depends on the Resurrection of Christ.

But it is very hard for human beings to believe that bodies corrupted and decayed will be resurrected. Even philosophers who have held the immortality of the soul have not accepted the resurrection of the body. Scripture has two remedies for our weakness: by directing us first to the Resurrection of Christ as the similitude of our own and then to the omnipotence of God. 'So often as resurrection is treated, let Christ's image come before us. He so passed through the course of his mortal life in the nature which he took of us that he has now obtained immortality and is a guarantee of our future resurrection . . . It is wrong to separate him from us. Nor is this possible without tearing him apart' (xxv.3, 435$^{3-7}$). Christ did not die and rise again as a private person, but for his people. The resurrection that was begun in the Head must be completed in the members. Certainly, there is a difference, in that Christ's body did not decay, whereas those of believers will. Nevertheless, 'Christ rose again in order to have us as his companions of the future life. He was raised by the Father in that he was the Head of the Church, from which he in no way allows himself to be torn away. He was raised by the power of the Spirit, who is also common to us for the office of giving life. Finally, he was raised that he might be the resurrection and the life' (xxv.3, 436$^{7-11}$).

If Christ's Resurrection is the guarantee of that of believers, it follows that we must be fully convinced that he really did rise from the dead. Calvin therefore sets out the New Testament evidence for Christ's Resurrection. This follows familiar lines and we need not detail the evidence.

The second scriptural remedy is that we should consider God's omnipotence. We shall only believe in our resurrection if we give God's power the honour it deserves. This concept is not treated metaphysically, but by examples from Scripture of God exercising his power in such wonderful instances of reviving as the quickening of the dry bones in Ezekiel 37.

It is in line with Calvin's teaching in Book I, chapter iii, that the knowledge of God is naturally implanted in all men's minds, that he can turn the flank of heathen hopelessness by pointing to the custom of burying the dead as a sort of picture of hope of resurrection, as 'a security of new life'. Those who practised burial had an image (*effigies*) of the resurrection before their eyes. Yet Satan corrupted even this image with various errors and so obscured its meaning. The Chiliasts, for example, in the early centuries of the Church, interpreted Revelation 20:1–5 as teaching that the reign of Christ would last for only 1,000 years. Scripture says clearly that there will be no end to the blessedness of the elect and to the punishment of the rejected. Christ's kingdom is everlasting.

Another error was the Anabaptist belief that at death both the body and soul die and that the souls are raised again with their bodies. Calvin reminds us that he has in fact already answered this error when writing on man as creature (I.xv.2) and shown that the soul is immortal and, therefore, does not die with the body. (He had combated these ideas before. First in his early work *De Psychopannychia* (1542),[8] *The Sleep of the Soul after Death*, and also in a letter to Socinus of 26 June 1549 (CO 13.309–311) which he used as the basis for paragraphs 7–8 of this chapter.) It is not right to enquire into the state or place of souls between death and the resurrection. It is sufficient to know that the souls of believers 'retire into blessed rest, where they await happily and joyfully the fruition of the promised glory' (xxv.6, 442^{31-33}).

Yet another error is that the bodies raised again are not those that died and decayed, but new and different bodies. The Manichees said that this was because the human body was inherently unclean, as created by the devil, and that, therefore, it was not fit to rise to eternal life. Calvin takes his stand on the superiority of grace over nature. Certainly, as sinful, human bodies are not fit for life or resurrection. But Scripture tells us that the bodies of believers are temples of the Holy Spirit and members of Christ, and that they belong to God. Moreover, Christ's body that rose from the tomb was the same that was crucified and died and laid in the tomb. But it has already been said that his Resurrection was the similitude of ours. Therefore, believers rise again with the same body that was theirs on earth. Calvin says he is ashamed to spend so long on such a straightforward subject, but it is one that worries people. In fact this error is the offspring not simply of wrong thinking, but of unbelief that God is able to work this miracle.

There is a yet more difficult question to consider: 'By what right is the resurrection, which is the unique blessing of Christ, common to the ungodly and those accursed by God?' (xxv.9, 451$^{5-7}$). The argument of the objection goes like this: in Adam all die; Christ came as the resurrection and the life; therefore, is not the whole human race given life indiscriminately? But it is inconsistent that obstinate unbelievers should receive what the godly recover by faith alone; yet Scripture teaches that there will be a resurrection to judgement and also to life.

Calvin's reply seems to be based, not on Scripture, but on analogy from daily experience. It was not only eternal life that Adam, and in him his descendants, forfeited, but the very means of existence, food and so forth. God provided these means in his kindness not only to the elect, but to all indiscriminately (though it was in order to make sinners the more inexcusable). Although sinners deserved immediate death and destruction, God provided an intermediate state 'so that outside life they might live in death' (xxv.9, 451^{31}). Resurrection drags unbelievers to the judgement seat of Christ. But the main emphasis in Scripture is on the resurrection to life, 'because properly speaking Christ did not come to destroy but to save the world. This is why in the Creed there is mention only of the blessed life' (xxv.9, 452$^{1-3}$).

Believers must, therefore, keep in their minds the eternal blessedness which is the aim of resurrection. The wonders of it are too great for us to grasp until the day when we shall see the Lord face to face. The greatest wonder of all is that it is not simply the enjoyment of blessings, but the enjoyment of God himself. All blessedness is contained in this, that 'the Lord shall share with the elect his glory, power, righteousness, nay, shall give them himself to be enjoyed and, what is even more excellent, shall in a certain manner grow into one with them' (xxv.10, 453$^{19-21}$). For the present, however, we must cultivate sobriety. We must not desire more than is lawful for us, must not speculate unlawfully. The rule is, once again, to follow Holy Scripture. People have indulged in all sorts of conjectures and speculations about the heavenly state; but they have been drawn deeper and deeper into a labyrinth, until at last there is no way for them to struggle out. We must be content with seeing 'in a glass darkly' (1 Cor 13:12) until we see face to face. 'As for me, I not only keep myself personally from the unnecessary investigation of unprofitable things, but I also consider that I should take care not to foster the levity of others by replying to it' (xxv.11, 454^{27-30}).

The final paragraph of this Book speaks with horror of the wretched state of the rejected in eternity. Scripture uses pictorial expressions to disturb and horrify us. The rejected are alienated from the society of God for ever and experience nothing but the terrible effects of his enmity and anger. Yet Calvin will not end on this fearsome note, but flies at once to the positive: 'Psalm 90 contains a memorable statement about this. Although [God] by his mere look overthrows all mortals and reduces them to nothing, yet he presses upon his servants in order that they may be fearful in this world; and he incites them to hasten on, laden with the cross, until he himself shall be all in all' (xxv.12, 456^{24-29}).

Notes

1   See R. S. Wallace, *Calvin's Doctrine of the Christian Life* (Edinburgh, 1959); W. Krusche, *Das Wirken des Heiligen Geistes nach Calvin* (Göttingen, 1957).

2   *intinctas*: literally, 'dipped in'; used by Tertullian for 'baptize' (*De paenitentia*, 6). Neither 'tinctured' (Allen) nor 'instilled' (Beveridge), nor 'steeped' (Battles) will do. Norton is right: 'our souls first washed with his holiness'.

3   H. Denzinger, rev. A. Schönmetzer, *Enchiridion Symbolorum* (Freiburg, 1965), pp. 368–81; Calvin, 'Antidote to the Council of Trent' in *Tracts and Treatises* (Grand Rapids, 1958), III, pp. 17–188 (CO 7, 365–506).

4   See a thorough account of the history from Augustine to Luther in H. J. McSorley, *Luther: Right or Wrong?* (New York, 1969) and the sketch in the essay 'Predestination' in A. Richardson (ed.), *A Dictionary of Christian Theology* (London, 1969), pp. 264–72. Karl Barth's radical criticisms of Calvin come in *Church Dogmatics* II/2 (Edinburgh, 1957).

5   Both texts in *Luther and Erasmus: Free Will and Salvation* (Library of Christian Classics vol. XVII, London, 1969).

6   J. B. Mozley, *A Treatise on the Augustinian Doctrine of Predestination* (London, 1878), p. 267n and Note XXI, pp. 393ff.

7   Martin Bucer, *Enarrationes in Euangelia* (1530), fol. 122a.

8   But written, it would seem, in 1534.

Part Four

Outward means

1 THE TRUE CHURCH[1]

Book IV of the *Institutio* corresponds to the fourth part of the Apostles' Creed: 'I believe . . . the holy catholic Church, the communion of saints, the forgiveness of sins'. (The final clauses, 'the resurrection of the body and the life everlasting', were the subject of the last chapter of the previous Book.) But this Book differs from the rest in that it is not a continuation of the argument sustained throughout Books I–III. It is rather a gathering up of the themes into their concrete realization in the believer's earthly life. The title makes this plain: *On the External Means or Helps by which God invites us into the Society of Christ and keeps us in it.* 'Society of Christ' is here primarily a synonym for union with Christ. Union with Christ is union with the one who is no longer on earth but in heaven. It is effected by the secret inward work of the Spirit. But the Spirit uses earthly means to bring this to pass. He uses ordinary words spoken by human tongues; he uses water; he uses bread and wine. The elect are called by the preaching of the Gospel, sealed by Baptism, nurtured by the Lord's Supper, and thus brought into and kept in the society of Christ. 'Society of Christ' is now seen to be also a synonym for 'the Church'.

Calvin begins with a long treatise on the Church, occupying chapters i–xiii. First, without history or polemic, he sets out his understanding of the Church, and then underlines this by contrasting the true Church with the false. A chapter on the ministry of the Church comes next, followed by an account of the history of the ministry and of Church government in the early centuries. In chapters v–vii is considered the burning question of the day, the break of the Reformers from Rome. In the early sixteenth century the word 'Church' meant for most people the single European Church owing allegiance to the Pope. The Reformers were, therefore, faced with the initial difficulty of persuading others that the word could be validly used without reference to Rome. In these chapters Calvin deals with the papal claim to primacy and government by the Papacy. This leads him on, in chapter viii, to the question of the Church's authority and thence to the authority of Councils and Church laws, with the same subject being dealt with in relation to 'the power of the keys' and Church discipline (chapters xi–xii). The final section in this part of the Book looks at the legitimacy and validity of vows.

We must limit ourselves to the positive teaching, as distinct from the polemic and historical.

The title of chapter i sets the scene: 'The True Church, with which Union must be cultivated, because she is the Mother of all the Godly'.

The three words with which the chapter opens are definitive for the whole understanding of the Church. They are: *Fide, Euangelii, Christum* – 'Faith, the Gospel, Christ'. In effect they summarize Books II and III. The full sentence runs: 'That by *the faith* of the *Gospel Christ* becomes ours and we become partakers of the salvation and eternal blessedness brought by him, was expounded in the previous Book' (IV.i.1, OS V.1[8–10]). But we are so weak and slothful that we need external helps if we are to reach the goal. In particular the Gospel must be kept alive and active. To this end God has deposited it to be kept safe by the Church and has appointed preachers and teachers of the Gospel, so that there may be a consensus of belief. He has also instituted the Sacraments, which will be 'more than useful helps to foster and confirm faith' (i.1, 1[20–21]).

But what is this 'Church' which is entrusted with the Gospel? At once the concept of motherhood appears: 'I will begin with the Church. In her bosom God wills to assemble his children, not only that they may be nourished by her work and ministry while they are babies and children, but that they may also be ruled by her maternal care until at last they grow up and come to the goal of faith [i.e., heaven]. For those things which God has joined together it is not lawful to separate. So that the Church is the mother of those of whom he is the Father' (i.1, 1[29]–2[2]).

The Creed comes into the open again. Calvin follows Augustine and Rufinus in omitting the preposition 'in', since one cannot say 'I believe in the Church' as one says 'I believe in God'. The significance of the confession 'I believe' here is that the Church is known and recognized only by faith. Only God knows those who are his own; it is his secret election which is the foundation of the Church. This election can, as we saw, be perceived only by faith. 'I believe the Church' is a judgement made from within the Church, not from outside.

The Church is called 'Catholic' or 'universal' because it is impossible to have more than one Church without Christ being torn apart. 'Catholic' is understood, not primarily in the sense of there being a world-wide Church, but as a statement of the Church's unity in the one Christ. Chosen in Christ, engrafted into him by calling through the Gospel, believers are one with him; and if one with him, then one with all others similarly chosen and engrafted into him. It would be absurd to imagine a conglomerate of warring factions within Christ who are yet in common harmony with him: 'depending on one Head, growing together into one as a body, they cohere in a mutual connection as members of the same body. They truly become one who live together in one faith, hope, and love by the same Spirit of God and are called not only into the same inheritance of eternal life but into participation of the one God and Christ' (i.2, 4$^{8-14}$).

'The communion of saints' expresses the quality of the Church. Believers are joined to the society of Christ so that they may communicate to one another all the benefits which God has bestowed on each in a rich diversity. Without infringing civil order and personal possession, all within this society, in which God is the common Father and Christ the common Head, are joined together in brotherly love and, therefore, communicate and share with one another.

Calvin takes up again the theme of personal election. We believe the Church 'so that we may be surely convinced that we are members of it' (i.3, 6$^{2-3}$). Our salvation stands, first, on God's choosing of us, which cannot change. God's choice is joined with the steadfastness of Christ, who will not allow his sheep to be plucked out of his hand. Next, the truth will always remain with us while we are kept in the bosom of the Church. And finally, we feel that God's promises about the Church belong to us – for example, 'God is in the midst of her [that is, Jerusalem, the type of the Church]; therefore shall she not be removed' (Ps 46:5).

But all this is a matter of faith. Not faith directly that we are elect and not rejected (direct perception is God's prerogative), but faith that those who are in Christ by God's mercy and through the work of the Holy Spirit are separated as God's own possession, the Church. Hence it is faith that, 'since we are of that number, we ourselves are participants in such great grace' (i.3, 7^{3-4}).

The Church is the 'mother' of all believers. Calvin now fills out the meaning of this metaphor: 'There is no other entry into life except she shall conceive us in her womb, bring us forth, nourish us at her breasts, and finally keep us under her care and governance until we put off this mortal flesh and become like the Angels' (i.4, 7^{7-10}) – a picturesque way of describing the Church proclaiming the Gospel, leading souls to repentance and faith, teaching, helping and governing them all the days of their earthly life. When Calvin turns the metaphor slightly, so that the mother becomes a school in which we must learn throughout our life, the image of motherhood is not completely left, but she is now become what previous ages called our *alma mater*, the mother of our souls or minds. It is the necessity for believers to belong to the Church that Calvin is chiefly emphasizing here. So necessary is it that 'outside her bosom there is no hope of remission of sins or any salvation' (i.4, 7^{13-14}). To separate from the Church is always fatal.

Scripture speaks of the Church in a twofold way. It presents the Church in its truth in God's sight. In this sense it consists only of those who are God's children by the grace of adoption, who are genuine members of Christ in the sense in which this has been explained in Book III. In this sense the Church consists of all the elect from the beginning of the world. But secondly, the Church in Scripture is shown in its earthly form. Now it is a question of men's activities. They profess to be believers in God and Christ, they are baptized, they share in the Lord's Supper, they agree in the genuine teaching of Scripture, they keep a form of ministry. Members of the Church in this sense are no longer to be equated with the true children of God by adoption and grace. The Church contains many hypocrites, many wicked, many ambitious for gain or status. It is this formal, visible, imperfect Church to which believers belong and to which they must keep.

A certain ambiguity has now been introduced into the picture of the Church. Not only does it lack the ultimate clarity and glory which leave no doubt that the Church of the elect really is the Church, but even on its own earthly level it is sometimes so deformed and weak that it is doubtful whether it really deserves to be called 'Church'. There is, of course, no problem from God's side. He knows his own. But we are often mistaken about men. Some seem good and genuine, only to fall completely away. Others who are a disgrace to the Church repent. In this regard our knowledge of the Church is not a perception by faith but has to be a 'judgement of charity'. We must acknowledge as fellow members those who profess God and Christ by 'the confession of faith, and example of life, and participation in the Sacraments' (i.8, 12$^{18-20}$).

There is also the question of the acknowledgement of the body as a whole. God has given certain marks by which a body can be recognized as the Church. They are the preaching of the Gospel and the administration of the two Sacraments instituted by Christ: 'For wherever we see God's Word being sincerely preached and heard, where the sacraments instituted by Christ are administered, there, we cannot possibly doubt, is the Church of God' (i.9, 13$^{24-29}$).

Why these two 'marks' should be the identification of the Church can easily be deduced from what Calvin has said about the Gospel and what in a later chapter he will say about the Sacraments. The Church is not merely a group of people sharing the same outlook, the same ideas, the same purposes, not even a body of people with a common faith, hope and love. The Church is the body united with its Head. It is Christ and his people as a unit. Hence it is the presence of Christ as the Head of the body that makes the body into the Church. But how is Christ present? Christ, the Word of God, is never to be separated from the Gospel, the message or word about the Word. If never to be separated, then he is present in the proclamation. When the Gospel is preached it is not a human declaration about an absent subject. The subject himself is present as the good news and its efficacy. Thus, to say that the preaching of the Gospel is the first mark of the Church is equivalent to saying that the Church is only the Church because Christ is present with his people, and that his presence is realized in the earthly form of proclamation. Similarly with the Sacraments of Baptism and the Lord's Supper. These are not merely signs pointing away to an absent Redeemer, but symbols in which the Redeemer is present. The Church is only the Church because Christ is present as Head of the body; and his presence is realized in the earthly forms of the Gospel and the Sacraments.

We may conceive of the Church as universal, assembled out of the various nations and yet at one in a general agreement of the truth of God's Word. Or we may conceive of the Church as local.

131

But each local Church has the right to be called 'Church' and each has the authority belonging to the Church. Obviously, it is to these local Churches that believers belong by their profession of faith. Some members are no doubt insincere; but they must be tolerated by their fellow members until they are removed by lawful authority. That unbelievers are members does not deprive a local Church of its Church-hood. That depends on whether the Gospel is preached and the two Sacraments administered.

But the Word is not preached and the Sacraments administered just to demonstrate that here is the Church. This would certainly be a piece of cold blasphemy. The purpose of these two 'symbols of the Church' is that souls may be saved, that the Church may be built up into the Lord's holy Temple. Nor can they fail to accomplish their purpose, not necessarily immediately but over a period of time, of conveying God's gracious blessing. This is why it is so wicked to leave the Church: 'A more atrocious crime cannot be imagined than to violate with faithless sacrilege the marriage which the only-begotten Son of God has condescended to contract with us' (i.10, 15$^{15-17}$). To leave the Church is to disown God and Christ.

Nevertheless, we must not be so rigorous as to deny Church-hood to any body which seems to us not perfectly pure and sound. A Church may have many faults and yet still be the Church. For there are two sorts of errors. There are the deadly errors, where, say, the unity of God, or the deity of Christ, or salvation by God's mercy alone are denied. With such bodies we should have no fellowship. But there are also disagreements about lesser points. The example Calvin chooses is one of the minor questions he had dealt with in the last chapter of Book III. Some say that after death souls go straight to heaven, whereas others hesitate to define a place but say that the souls live with the Lord. Such disagreements are not sufficient cause for separating from a Church.

Then there are the perfectionists of every age – the Donatists in the early Church, the Cathari in the Middle Ages, some Anabaptist groups in the sixteenth century. They imagine, he says scornfully, that they are already Angels in Paradise and despise the rest. They separate from the Church where even slight errors are to be seen. It is true that they are not all actuated by pride; many are simply over-enthusiastic. Nevertheless, it is wrong for them to forsake a Church because the life of some fellow member is imperfect. He points to the classic case of the Church at Corinth, which Paul still called 'the Church' in spite of its quite appalling sins.

Although separation sometimes comes from excess of zeal, the hypercritical spirit that motivates it arises out of pride, contempt, and a false view of holiness. This is most often true of the ringleaders. They ought to realize that

> many are truly holy and innocent in God's eyes whom they fail to discern. Let them reflect that many who seem to be sick are not at all happy or pleased with their faults but are repeatedly stirred by an earnest fear of the Lord to aspire after greater purity. Let them reflect that a man is not to be judged from one action; for sometimes even the holiest fall very grievously. Let them reflect that in gathering a Church the ministry of the Word and the participation of the holy Mysteries is too weighty for it to vanish because of the guilt of the ungodly. (i.16, 20^{31}–21^2)

Calvin adds that the Prophets did not separate from the Church in spite of the great sins of Israel and Judah, and that Christ and his Apostles did not separate from the Church governed by the Pharisees and Sadducees, but worshipped in the Temple.

The separatists want a Church without the slightest blemish. Certainly, we should press towards perfection; but to trust to perfection here on earth 'I say is a devilish invention' (i.20, 23^{28-29}). In the Creed 'I believe . . . in the forgiveness of sins' is joined to the clause on the Church. God's mercy and forgiveness are promised only to those who are in the communion of saints. This is why entry into the Church is by Baptism, the washing from uncleanness by God's goodness. But it is not only a question of entry into the Church, but also of the continuing daily pardon for the many infirmities of its members. The sins of believers are remitted by the ministers of the Church 'when Priests or Bishops, to whom this office is committed, confirm godly consciences in the hope of pardon and remission by the Gospel promises; and that either publicly or privately as need demands' (i.22, 25^{16-22}). The Anabaptists, like the Donatists, believe that after they are baptized they are born again to a pure and angelic life without sin. Hence they regard post-Baptismal sin as unforgivable, because only the first remission is valid.

In chapter ii, 'A Comparison of the False Church with the True', 'the false Church' is no longer the Anabaptists, but the Papacy. Calvin has gone to great lengths to reject puritanical separatism. But there is a limit to toleration. When 'the sum of necessary doctrine' is overturned and the use of the Sacraments is corrupted, the Church collapses, 'like a man with his throat cut or his heart mortally wounded' (ii.1, 31^{8-9}). The foundation of the Church is the teaching of the Prophets and Apostles, calling us to trust in Christ alone. Take that away and the Church falls.

But this, for Calvin, is precisely the case with the Papacy. In place of the ministry of the Word of God, it has a perverted form of Church government as well as many errors; in place of the Lord's Supper the sacrilegious celebration of the Mass. Its worship is deformed by superstitions; true doctrine either buried under accretions or completely driven away. Its claim to Church-hood is an appeal to antiquity and to succession of ministry from the Apostles. But any succession must consist in faithfulness to the teaching of the originals if it is to be valid. Therefore, the case between the Papacy and the Reformers must be judged by which side can be shown to be obedient to the teaching of Christ, who called those his sheep who listened to his voice (John 10:3, 16) and who governs his Church by his Word.

The Romanists accuse us, says Calvin, of heresy and schism. And, indeed, cannot the arguments against the separatists be turned back on the Reformers? Schism, however, must be defined. It has already been laid down that the Church is known by whether it preaches the Gospel and administers the Sacraments according to Christ's institution, since these are the indications as to whether Christ is present and, therefore, forms the Church. Hence schism means departing from Christ the Head of the Church. We, on the contrary, 'had to leave them in order that we might come to Christ' (ii.6, 37^{35-36}). In regard to agreement within the Church, Cyprian said the true word that the fount of agreement is 'the unique episcopacy of Christ'. Christ is the sole Bishop, the sole Governor of his Church. He rules and governs it by his Word.

Yet it seems unrealistic to say that there are no individual Churches under the Papacy. Calvin does not deny that traces of Church-hood remain. God's faithfulness to his promise is never blotted out by the unfaithfulness of men. In Christian Europe God preserved under the Papacy Baptism, the testimony of God's Covenant, as well as what Calvin loosely calls 'other remnants'. (We should recall that the Reformers were all baptized, as infants, by Romanist priests and were not rebaptized when they left the Papacy.) Thus the Church in Europe was not completely destroyed from the foundations up; God allowed 'a half-ruined edifice to remain' (ii.11, 41^{23-24}).

The argument does not turn on whether some local bodies under the Papacy were Churches or not, but whether the whole constitution is recognizable as the true and legitimate Church. It is this that Calvin is denying. But even to concede that there are local Churches among them can only be done with the caveat that they have been corrupted by the system as a whole and cannot be regarded formally as Churches: 'I say that they are Churches so far as the Lord wonderfully preserves these remnants of his people, although wretchedly scattered and ruined, and so far as the symbols of the Church remain . . . But because on the other hand those marks which we ought especially to consider in this dispute are blotted out, I say that each assembly and the whole body lack the legitimate form of the Church' (ii.12, 42[10–17]).

It is clear from this chapter not only why the various Reformers or national Churches left the Papacy, but also why, as Calvin has told us elsewhere, he himself had such a struggle to take this step, so highly did he rank the Church and so strongly did he identify the Church with the Papacy. When, however, he had decided that what he had from childhood regarded as the Church could not be granted the name, he left it 'to come to Christ', to join those bodies where Christ was present in the preaching of the Word and the administration of the dominical Sacraments.

2   THE CHURCH'S MINISTRY

When Calvin enters on his discussion of 'The Doctors [i.e., teachers] and Ministers of the Church, their Election and Office' he lays the emphasis on the ministry as a tool wielded by the hand of the Lord. It is the word 'Lord' that is stressed in the first sentence. 'We must now speak of the order by which *the Lord* wishes his Church to be directed' (iii.1, 42[20–21]). He alone rules and reigns over the Church, exercising his rule only by the Word. But because he is not visibly present with his people he makes use of the ministry of men as a sort of 'vicarious activity', a phrase Calvin explains as God using a tool like a workman. God could do this work directly, without the human tools, or he could use Angels to do it; but it is for the Church's advantage that he should use human ministry. For one thing it shows God's benevolence in so honouring men; for another it demands humility in those who must submit themselves to fellow men who may even be their inferiors; and, lastly, it binds the Church together in mutual charity and unity. It is the ministry which is the chief agent in making and maintaining unity, 'the chief sinew by which believers are united in one body' (iii.2, 44$^{16-17}$). The gifts which God gives to men he gives through the ministry; but more than gifts, he gives himself by the power of the Spirit.

His scriptural platform here is Ephesians 4:8–12: 'When he ascended up on high he led captivity captive and gave gifts to men. He that descended is the same that ascended that he might fill all things. And he gave some [to be] Apostles, and some Prophets, and some Evangelists, and some Pastors and Doctors, for the renewal of the saints, for the work of administration, for the building up of the body of Christ.'

The ministers mentioned here are four in number (taking the last two as one): Apostles; Prophets; Evangelists; Pastors and Doctors. The first three Calvin regarded as temporary, belonging to 'the beginning of Christ's kingdom'. Apostles were, with the exception of Matthias, appointed directly by Christ to preach the Gospel to every creature. They were not limited by locality, but were sent to the whole world. Prophets Calvin takes in the New Testament context to be those with the office of interpreting God's will according to the special revelations they received. This office has also ceased, or at least is less evident. Evangelists were inferior in rank to the Apostles, but stood next to them and acted as their proxies, as Timothy and Titus for Paul.

Although Calvin judges these offices to be temporary, he does not exclude the possibility that God might sometimes, in cases of extreme need, use men in an apostolic or evangelistic way: 'I do not deny that God has sometimes raised up Apostles subsequently, or at least, Evangelists in their stead, as has happened in our own day (for there was great need for such to call the Church back from the defection of AntiChrist)' (iii.4, 46$^{26-29}$). These clauses refer primarily to Luther, as we learn from an earlier version of chapter xvii.32, where he calls him 'an outstanding Apostle of Christ' (390^{33}). Nevertheless, the office is not usual but extraordinary.

The last pair, Pastors and Doctors, the Church can never lack. Together constituting one office, the distinction between them is that Doctors are limited to being interpreters of Scripture, to preserve sound doctrine, whereas Pastors not only interpret Scripture (i.e., in preaching), but also administer the Sacraments and Church discipline. The Doctors correspond to the Prophets of Ephesians 4:11. The Prophets were superior to Doctors because of their unique gift of revelation, 'but the office of Doctor was almost the same in method and quite identical in aim' (iii.5, 47$^{6-8}$). The continuing office of Pastor corresponds to the temporary office of Apostle. Etymologically all ministers can be called 'Apostles' in that they are *sent* to proclaim the Gospel. But the word belongs particularly to the New Testament Apostles, who declared 'something new and unheard' (iii.5, 47[14]). Nevertheless, Pastors, apart from the fact that they have a local and not a world-wide sphere of activity, have the same province as the Apostles.

The province appears in the sending of the Twelve. Christ commanded them to do two things, according to Matthew 28:19: to preach the Gospel and to baptize those that believed, so that their sins might be forgiven. But he had already, at the Last Supper, commanded them 'to distribute the sacred symbols of his body and blood, according to his example. See how a sacred, inviolable and perpetual rule (*legem*) is imposed on those who succeed to the place of the Apostles!' (iii.6, 47[27]–48[3]). From this we learn how *the Lord* wishes his Church to be governed. The Apostles and their successors the Pastors are commanded to preach the Gospel, to baptize and to administer the Lord's Supper.

That a Pastor is appointed to one Church should not be interpreted rigidly. He can help out, as we say, when another Church is in need. But in general each Pastor has his own flock and has no right to interfere in other flocks. This is more than a sensible arrangement; it is God's order for his Church. Since this is so, Pastors should regard themselves as bound to their own Church. Yet Calvin is anxious to avoid rigidity and perhaps also wishes to distance himself from the relationship between the mediaeval parish and the feudal system, for he goes on, using the traditional legal terms, to say 'not that [the Pastor is], so to say, "bound to the soil" (*glebae addictus*) as the lawyers have it – that is, enslaved and so to say stuck fast, unable to move a foot' (iii.7, 49[24–26]). The Pastor is not an ecclesiastical serf. Yet he should not remove from his cure of his own will, and can only be moved to another Church by lawful authority.

The terms used for this office in the New Testament are four: Bishops, Priests (I have kept this rendering of *presbyter* rather than the English 'presbyter'. 'Priest' is merely in this context a short version of the same word. We should, of course, not take it in the context of sacrificial priesthood. The first English translation of the *Institutio* also used the word 'priests' here), Pastors and Ministers. They all refer to the same office. Other offices are mentioned in Romans 12:7–8 and 1 Corinthians 12:28. These are 'powers': gifts of healing, interpreting tongues, government and the care of the poor. 'Governors I reckon to be elders [*seniores*, not *presbyteri*] chosen from the people, who, together with the Bishops, should have charge of judging morals and administering discipline' (iii.8, 50^{21-23}). Nothing should be more diligently observed than Church order and there is no greater danger than disorderliness.

Yet another New Testament office is introduced with the care of the poor, which is committed to deacons. There are two 'degrees' of deacons, referring respectively to the administration of almsgiving and to the actual care of the sick and needy (i.e., by doctors, nurses, and so on).

As for the calling and appointment of the various ministers, four points must be observed: who should be appointed; in what way; by whom; and with what rites.

Individuals should heed their own consciences as to whether they are free from vices like ambition and avarice and have 'a sincere fear of God and intention to build up the Church' (iii.11, 52^{26-27}). But those who choose ministers must see whether the candidates are fit and suitable; 'because learning joined with *pietas* and the other gifts of a good Pastor are a sort of preparation for [the office]. For whom the Lord destines for such an office he first gives the weapons they need to fulfil it' (iii.11, 52^{33-36}).

In what way ministers should be chosen refers to the spirit in which they should be chosen. The fasting and prayers on such occasions in Acts show that there must be reverence, carefulness and seeking the guidance of the Spirit to choose aright.

It is not possible to learn from the example of the Apostles how Bishops and Pastors should be chosen, for their choosing was directly by Christ and therefore extraordinary, whereas Bishops must be chosen by human beings. But is this to be by the whole local Church, or by colleagues together with elders, or simply by one man? Calvin's opinion is that 'from the Word of God it is a lawful calling of a minister when those who seem to be fit are appointed by the consent and approval of the people, and the other Pastors should rule over the election lest things should be done amiss either by levity or wrong intentions or by tumult from the mob' (iii.15, 56^{15-18}).

Finally, the only rite used by the Apostles was the laying-on of hands. This Calvin regards as stemming from the Hebrew manner of blessing and consecrating and, therefore, as having the same general intention; that is, that ordination is a consecrating and offering to God of the man for the particular office. Since it was the usual method in the New Testament it should certainly be continued, even though it was not directly commanded. It is a useful symbol which both commends the dignity of the ministry to the people and also admonishes the one ordained that he is now not his own but is 'bound in servitude to God and the Church' (iii.16, 57^{11-12}). Nor is it an empty sign, so long as it is not used superstitiously. There is no need for the whole congregation to lay their hands on the ordinand; it is sufficient if the Pastors alone do this.

With the Apostles, and therefore with the Bishops and Pastors, is placed the ministry of forgiveness through faith in the Gospel which they proclaim. It is here that we find the heart of Calvin's doctrine of the Church. Ecclesiastical law or polity, organization, reform and removal of abuses, all these are means to serve the one end, the forgiveness and sanctification of sinners. All too often historians have dealt with Calvin's teaching and practice on the Church as if he were demonstrating theories as to how a well-organized Church should be run. It is cold and weak to speak of it in terms of 'the government of the Church' as if it were some sixteenth-century bureaucracy. The Pastors were there to bring their people to the knowledge of God through the forgiveness of their sins. Calvin himself, as a Pastor in Geneva, was dealing with men and women in inward trouble, with bad consciences. Practically every morning he was in the pulpit telling them that they were sinners for whom Christ had died and that they might live the lives of those forgiven. The teaching in the *Institutio* should be taken in this way.

We can see the Church order in practice in Geneva during Calvin's ministry there. The republic of Geneva consisted of the city itself and a few satellite villages. The form of Church order was drawn up in the *Ecclesiastical Ordinances* of 1541 by a committee of ministers and laymen, in which Calvin was the dominant (but sometimes overruled!) theologian. It established the four orders of ministry, together with their functions and appointments.

The city was divided into three parishes with a set quota of services – first thing in the morning and three o'clock in the afternoon on Sundays, as well as on Mondays, Wednesdays and Fridays, at the principal church, St Pierre. These weekday services were, after some fluctuation, settled several years later as a daily service. Baptisms were to be held at the regular services – apparently on Sundays, from the entries in the registers. Weddings were to be at the convenience of the couple, but this was frequently on Sundays, for the registers often record that Calvin celebrated one or more weddings at one of the Sunday services. There was also to be the Church for younger children, a 'catechism' to be held at noon in all three parish churches and to which all citizens were ordered to send their children.

The order of Doctors was responsible for education in Geneva, not only religious education, but also the necessary preparation in the form of languages and the subjects usually taught in the 'arts' courses at universities. Schools were set up for younger boys and girls, with the Collège on an advanced level corresponding to the current undergraduate courses at universities. In 1559 the Collège became the Academy, providing a full university education from professors in Old and New Testaments, Hebrew, Greek and mathematics. The intention was to furnish both the State and the Church with competent staff.

The third order, that of Elders, was disciplinary: 'Their office is to watch over the life of each person, to admonish in a friendly manner those whom they see to be at fault and leading a disorderly life and when necessary to report them to the Company [of Pastors] who will be authorized to administer fraternal discipline and to do so in association with the elders.'[2] The emphasis is on friendliness and brotherly help. Only those who were stubborn in their faults were to be punished by rebuke or, more seriously, by being reported to the City Council, which would, if the case were proved, administer more severe punishment.

The fourth order, that of Deacons, was divided into the finance group, receiving and administering funds for the hospital, the workhouse, the isolated plague-house and the hospice for travellers (Geneva lay on well-used trade routes), and those who actually cared for the sick and needy.

3 THE CHURCH'S AUTHORITY

It has become clear that the Church possesses a certain authority over its members (the word Calvin consistently uses is *potestas*). This *potestas* rests partly with individual Bishops and partly with Councils, whether general or provincial. The scope of the *potestas* lies in determining doctrine, in proposing laws and in judging morals. Calvin is careful to make clear that the autonomy of the State is in no way infringed by the Church's authority. This is spiritual, not civil, authority.

The first area of authority is the power to determine and explain what the Church believes. The purpose is constructive, to build up the Church in the Faith; it must never be conceived of or used destructively. Ministers are the servants of Christ and of the people for Christ's sake. If, therefore, Christ is the Lord, he must be allowed to have his authority, for he is 'the unique Teacher and Master of the Church' (viii.1, 134⁴).

It is not strictly true that the authority of teaching was committed to the Priests, Prophets, Apostles and their successors. Rather it was granted 'to the Word, the ministry of which was committed to them' (viii.2, 134¹⁷⁻¹⁸). They were not to bring forward 'anything of their own', but to speak only what they had first been told. And Calvin shows from many Old Testament passages that this was so for Moses, the Priests and the Prophets.

Nor were the Apostles in any different position. According to Matthew 28:19 they were to teach only what Christ had taught them. Their message was, therefore, not theirs but Christ's: 'He who was always the Father's unique and eternal Counsellor, appointed by the Father to be Lord and Teacher of all, prescribed to all ministers by his example in carrying out the ministry of teaching what rule should be followed' (viii.4, 136¹⁸⁻²²). Hence the Church is not autonomous nor its authority unlimited. It is subordinate to the Word of God so thoroughly that it is enclosed by the Word on all sides. The Church's only authority lies in the authority of Holy Scripture.

This rule was, says Calvin, operative from mankind's very creation, although the manner in which God's truth was learned varied. The truth itself was always the same, that God was known only in Christ ('no man knoweth the Father but the Son and he to whom the Son wills to reveal him' – Matt 11:27). Old Testament men knew God only as they saw him in Christ: 'I mean that God never revealed himself to men in any other way than through his Son, that is, his unique Wisdom, Light, and Truth. It was from this source that Adam, Noah, Abraham, Isaac, Jacob, and the rest, drew all they held of heavenly doctrine' (viii.5, 137¹⁰⁻¹⁴).

The knowledge was derived in various ways. With the patriarchs it was by 'secret revelations' confirmed by signs (Calvin is thinking, for example, of the rainbow in Gen 9:12ff.). They handed on to their descendants what they had been shown, and those descendants 'knew that what they were hearing came from heaven and not from earth because God inwardly declared it to them (*Deo intus dictante*)' (viii.6, 137²²⁻²³). At a later stage it was God's will that his Word should be written down, so that there should be an authoritative document in which the Priests could find what they were to teach the people, and which could also be the criterion of every-thing that was taught. This document is the Law, comprising the Pentateuch. Next came the Prophets. They added nothing to the Law apart from specific predictions, but were only interpreters of the Law, so that their teaching flowed from it and was related to it. According to God's will their teaching also was written down. The historical books should be taken with the Prophets, as also the Psalms. Thus under the old Covenant 'the Word of God' meant the corpus of Law, Prophets, histories and Psalms 'to whose rule the Prophets and Doctors up to the coming of Christ were bound to measure their teaching' (viii.6, 138[16–17]).

'But when at last the Wisdom of God was manifested in the flesh, he related plainly and clearly whatever the human mind can comprehend and ought to think about the heavenly Father. And so now, from the time when Christ the Sun of righteousness shone forth, we have the perfect brightness of Divine Truth, like the clear light of midday when before there had been twilight' (viii.7, 138[28–33]). Christ is the complete and final revelation of God; therefore, 'hear ye him!' (Matt 17:5). His Apostles had precisely the same duty as the Old Testament Prophets – to expound the Law and show that it was fulfilled in Christ. But, whereas the Prophets looked to a Christ yet to come, the Apostles could point to the Christ who had come and with whom they had lived and who had taught them. Their recognition of Christ was not by human percep-tion, it came 'by Christ's Spirit leading them and in a sense dictating their words' (viii.8, 140[5–6]).

The purpose of this piece of biblical literary criticism was to fix the authority of the Pastors, by whatever name called. In every-thing they were to be led by the Word of God. There was, to be sure, a difference between the Apostles and their successors in every age, in that the Apostles were 'sure and certain amanuenses of the Holy Spirit and that therefore their writings are to be held as the oracles of God' (viii.9, 141[12–13]). The successors of the Apostles may teach only what is declared and witnessed in these oracles.

To place the Church's authority in the Councils on the ground that they are ruled directly by the Holy Spirit, as Rome does, is, says Calvin, simply to say in effect that the Church is ruled by itself. For the Councils were composed of Bishops who governed the Church, which through them made new dogmas of faith.

This being a large subject, a new chapter is devoted to it. Calvin declares his own respect, even veneration, for Church Councils. But they should not be so revered that Christ's own rights are infringed. As the Head of the Church he has the right to preside at (or, to use the modern word, to be Chairman of) every council, and that without anyone else being his co-chairman. But how does Christ preside in his Church? It is not sufficient to say that the Spirit presides, for he is the Spirit of Christ and works through the Word. Hence, 'I say that Christ presides only when he governs the whole assembly by his Word and Spirit' (ix.1, 151$^{10-11}$). Councils are not in some privileged position of being exempt from subjection to God's Word, the teaching of Scripture. Matthew 18:20 is definitive for them also: 'where two or three are gathered together in my name, there am I in the midst of them.' 'In my name' means being content with and obedient to Holy Scripture alone. We have already seen that Christ is present with his people as the subject of the Word.

The second part of the authority of the Church consists in the power to make or introduce laws. Calvin considers this largely in terms of the individual conscience: 'we must now treat of whether the Church may bind consciences by its laws' (x.1, 164$^{14-15}$). Here it is a question of worshipping and serving God in the way that he himself has prescribed and of preserving spiritual liberty towards God. Calvin is not against regulations intended for discipline or public morality or peace and concord. It is when 'human traditions' concerning the worship and service of God go beyond or outside God's Word that they must be resisted. Christian freedom means that believers can have peace with God only if they are freed by Christ: 'If they want to keep the grace they once obtained in Christ, let them acknowledge one only King, their Liberator, Christ, and be ruled by one law of liberty, the holy Word of the Gospel. Let them not be kept in servitude; let them not be bound by any chains' (x.1, 165$^{6-10}$).

In the chapter on Christian liberty, Calvin had made the distinction between 'the external forum' and 'the forum of conscience'. Now he defines 'conscience'. When one apprehends something intellectually one is said 'to know' (*scire*). From *scire* comes *scientia* ('knowledge'), and from *scientia*, *con-scientia*, which implies a certain agreement of knowledge with another. 'So when they have an awareness of Divine judgement as, so to say, a witness attached to them which does not allow them to hide their sins but hales them as guilty before his judgement seat, that awareness is called "conscience". It is a certain medium between God and man' (x.3, 166$^{10-15}$). Whereas a man's outward activities are related to other men, conscience is related only to God. This being so, human laws which bind religious observances on consciences as necessary are unlawful, for conscience is Godward, not manward, and God is the sole Legislator in things pertaining to himself. Nothing can be added to his Law for men to live a good and holy life.

Good laws and customs for religious observance have their basis in Scripture and, therefore, carry God's authority. Calvin is thinking of such customs as kneeling to pray. But God has not laid down details of ceremony and behaviour at worship, and these can be changed as needs change. They can be observed with a free conscience and without superstition: 'What! is religion a matter of a woman's head-shawl, so that it is wicked to go out bareheaded? Or cannot the holy decree about her keeping silence be violated without criminality? Or is there some mystery in kneeling down . . . so that it cannot be omitted without guilt? Not at all! If a woman is in such a hurry to help a neighbour that she has no time to put on her hat, she is not wicked in running out bareheaded. And there are times when it is as opportune for her to speak as to be silent. Nor is there anything to stop a man standing to pray, if he cannot bend his knees through some disease' (x.31, 193$^{18-26}$). On the other hand, we should not deliberately break established Church customs if they are harmless.

The third and chief part of the Church's authority is its judicial authority. Just as the State needs civil power and authority and has a more or less sophisticated system of police and courts, so also the Church has jurisdiction in regard to the discipline of morals among its members. From the beginning the Church had courts 'to act as censors of morals, to investigate vices, and to govern by exercising the office of the keys' (xi.1, 195$^{14-16}$). In New Testament days the Sanhedrin was the Jewish court. Its authority, the *ius synedrii*, was transferred to the Church in the form of 'the power of the keys'. ('I will give unto thee the keys of the kingdom of heaven: and whatsoever thou shalt bind on earth shall be bound in heaven: and whatsoever thou shalt loose on earth shall be loosed in heaven' (Matt 16:19). Peter, to whom the promise was made, was regarded not as an individual, but as the representative of the apostolic body.)

To Matthew 16:19 should be joined John 20:23: 'Whosesoever sins ye remit, they are remitted unto them; and whosesoever sins ye retain, they are retained'. These passages Calvin interpreted, in agreement with his fellow Reformers, as the declaration of the Gospel message of forgiveness. 'For the sum of the Gospel is that all the slaves of sin and death are released and set free by the redemption which is in Christ Jesus. What is this but that all those who neither accept nor acknowledge Christ as their Liberator and Redeemer are condemned and damned to eternal chains?' (xi.1, 196[24–28]). Again, in reference to John 20:23, Calvin says that the Apostles have no other function than to be ministers of Christ, who spoke by their mouths. When they declared forgiveness by faith in him, he himself was declaring that the sins were forgiven: similarly with the declaration of condemnation. Hence the power of the keys rests in the preaching of the Gospel and, strictly speaking, did not belong to the Apostles and their successors, but with God's Word declared by them.

Matthew 16:19 has a wider reference than the Johannine passage, in that it concerns not only preaching, but also the discipline of excommunication. Excommunication is 'binding' in the sense of condemning a man's life and morals and warning him that he will be eternally lost if he does not repent. 'Loosing' is receiving a penitent again into communion. Even in this word 'ex-communication' Calvin is stressing the theme of union with Christ. Ex-communication is placing the unrepentant sinner outside communion with his fellow members and with Christ. Receiving again into communion 'as it were makes him participant of the unity which [the Church] has in Christ Jesus' (xi.2, 198[15–16]).

Chapter xii deals at greater length with this subject. In leaving the Papacy, the Reformers were faced with the problem of the form of the Church in its many aspects. Rome had exercised a strict rule over clergy and laity, centred, so far as general morals go, in the Sacrament of penance, with its steps of confession, contrition, absolution and satisfaction. It was clear to Calvin from Scripture that some form of discipline was not merely desirable but necessary. He even went so far, in a letter of 1540,[3] as to say that it would be better to keep the current system unless a better could be substituted. In the event he evolved the discipline which he put into practice in Geneva.

He first speaks in general of the necessity and scope of discipline, which largely depends on the power of the keys and the spiritual jurisdiction of the Church. It is closely related to preaching, indeed it is a subjunct of it. If the teaching of the Word of God is the soul of the Church, then discipline is the ligaments that hold the body together. To this image Calvin adds others: 'Discipline is like a bridle by which those who fight against Christ's teaching are checked and turned. Or it is like a goad to stir up the unwilling. Sometimes also it is like a fatherly rod with which those who fall more grievously are mercifully chastised in proportion to the gentleness of Christ's Spirit' (xii.1, 212^{31}–213^5). Whatever the metaphor, discipline is always intended as the specific application of the general preaching of the Gospel. It is meant to give an opportunity for private admonitions, which are specifically the task of Pastors and Priests (but can be given by anybody), who should not only preach in public but also warn and exhort people at home. Discipline gives an added force and authority to preaching when people are slow to obey.

Matthew 18:15ff. provides the framework for the administration of discipline. The first step should be a private approach to the one going astray. If this fails, the next step is to warn him in the presence of witnesses. Finally, the case of a stubborn offender is to be referred to the Church court, where he will receive a graver warning. If after this he perseveres in his wickedness, he is 'to be rejected from the society of believers' (xii.2, 213^{32}).

The three purposes of correction and excommunication are: first, to remove the insult offered to God of flagrant and deliberate sinners being called Christians. For the Church is the body of Christ; to condone sin is to disgrace the Head of the body. Moreover, to admit flagrant sinners to the Lord's Supper is to profane that holy Institution. Ex-communication is banishment from communicating. Secondly, as Paul says in 1 Corinthians 5:11, the good must be kept from contamination by the bad. And thirdly, in regard to the offender himself, the purpose is that he shall repent and be restored.

What must never be neglected is that necessary severity is always to be joined with a spirit of kindness. The purpose of discipline is not to destroy, but to save by bringing a sinner to repentance. When it is seen that the sinner is penitent there should be no more pressure on him. The early Church, apart from one or two fathers, was too rigorous. Sinners were driven to despair by being sentenced to long periods of excommunication. The trigger-happy use of excommunication by the contemporary (to Calvin) Papacy is altogether wrong.

Excommunication must not be confused with election and rejection. 'It is not for us to expunge from the number of the elect those who are expelled from the Church, or to despair of them as already lost. Certainly, it is right to regard them as aliens from the Church and therefore from Christ – but only for as long as they remain separated' (xii.9, 220^{10-14}). Even if they continue in disobedience we must commit them to God's judgement and go on praying for them. Excommunication is not a matter of consigning men to eternal destruction; that rests with God alone. All we may do is to judge according to God's revealed Law. Nor must we limit God's mercy: 'whenever it seems good to him, the worst are turned into the best, the aliens are ingrafted, the outsiders adopted into the Church' (xii.9, 220$^{24-26}$). Excommunication is to be distinguished from *anathema* or curse. This does indeed consign a sinner to eternal ruin. But it is used very rarely indeed.

As a corollary to the purpose of excommunication, Calvin warns believers not to be on intimate terms with excommunicated persons, yet at the same time always to strive to help them and lead them to repentance. Unless such kindness is shown by the rest of the Church members, there will be the danger of discipline degenerating into slaughter.

This is the main part of Calvin's teaching on discipline. For the rest he deals with the occasional biddings to fasting and special days of prayer. All such things have always been practised in the Church and were taken from the Old Testament Law and Prophets. But they are occasional, as circumstances demand. The times, methods and forms are not laid down in Scripture, but are left to the discretion of the Church.

4 THE SACRAMENTS

(i) General[4]

The opening words of chapter xiv ('On the Sacraments') are 'The preaching of the Gospel'. Calvin is indicating that the Sacraments are not a separate or independent means by which God invites us into and keeps us in the society of Christ, but are intimately related to the preaching of the Gospel. We have heard that it is the preaching of the Word and the administration of the Sacraments that identify a body as being the Church of God. But although the Sacraments are not independent of the Word they are, nevertheless, plainly not identical with preaching and, therefore, need to be considered in themselves. Hence the first sentence goes on to call the Sacraments 'another help akin to the preaching of the Gospel' (258$^{33-34}$). They are 'akin' yet 'another'.

The terms of reference that Calvin sets for the discussion are, first, 'For what purpose the Sacraments were instituted', and, secondly, 'What is their present use?' But the initial step is to explain their nature. A Sacrament is 'an external symbol by which the Lord seals in our consciences the promises of his goodwill towards us; [this is] to sustain the weakness of our faith. And [in them] we on our side testify our *pietas* towards him both before him and the Angels and also before men' (xiv.1, 259$^{2-6}$). This can be put even more concisely as 'a testimony of the Divine grace towards us confirmed by an external sign, with a mutual confirmation of our *pietas* towards him' (xiv.1, 259$^{8-10}$). All of which, says Calvin, is another way of putting Augustine's well-known definition of 'the visible sign of a holy entity' or 'the visible form of an invisible grace' – but this is ambiguous from its brevity.

As he begins to build up his exposition, Calvin relates it firmly to the Gospel. There cannot be a Sacrament apart from what God has promised. The Sacrament acts as an appendix to the promise, confirming it and making it in a sense certain to us. This does not mean that the Word of promise is in any way weak and needs strengthening. What is weak is our faith in the promise. The Sacraments are intended to establish our weak faith in the firm and faithful promise of God. This they are qualified to do as being on our own level, earthly signs for earthly creatures. They have the same 'message' as the Gospel, and indeed are constituted of the Word and the sign, so that the promise declared by the preacher 'leads the people by the hand to where the sign points and directs us' (xiv.4, 262$^{1-2}$).

Not all Calvin's theological friends were happy with the place he gave to the Sacraments in the order of salvation. If you believe God's Word, what need have you of the Sacraments as secondary aids to salvation? Calvin replies with analogies: a seal attached to an official document is nothing in itself and adds nothing to the substance of the document. But it does confirm that document to us as being authentic. He goes further: Sacraments have a certain quality not possessed by the Word 'in that they represent these things to the life for us, as if they were painted on a canvas' (xiv.5, 262$^{23-24}$). There is a difference between an action described in words and a faithful picture of it. The believer is not held fast by the material spectacle when he thinks of the Sacraments, but 'he rises by those analogies which I have indicated to the sublime mysteries hidden in the Sacraments' (xiv.5, 262$^{31-34}$).

There are, after all, many sacramental acts in daily life – shaking hands, for example, on reaching an agreement. The action is not itself the agreement, but symbolizes the agreement. Calvin reminds us that Augustine called the Sacraments 'visible words', and repeats his painting metaphor. A Sacrament 'represents God's promises as if they were painted on a canvas and he sets them in our sight expressed pictorially (*graphicè*) and in imagery (*eikonikōs*)' (xiv.6, 263[15–17]).

The friendly critics fell back on Philip's statement to the Ethiopian eunuch: 'If thou believest with all thy heart, thou mayest [be baptized]' (Acts 8:37). If the heart is filled with faith, what need is there of Sacraments to confirm the faith? Calvin explains that 'with all thy heart' is a common biblical term for 'wholeheartedly', meaning 'sincerely', not 'perfectly'. For is not a large part of all our hearts empty of faith and needing a daily increase?

The order of salvation is, first, that the Lord teaches and trains his people by means of the preaching of the Word; secondly, that he confirms the preaching to us by means of the Sacraments; and thirdly, that he illuminates our minds by the light of the Holy Spirit and thus opens an entrance for the Word and the Sacraments. It is the Spirit who gives both Word and Sacraments their power. There is no 'secret force' inherent in the Sacraments themselves which will avail to confirm our faith. They are efficacious only when the Spirit is present as the inward teacher. All the power is with the Spirit, the Sacraments have only the ministry.

Calvin next denies two opposing views of the Sacraments. Zwingli had concentrated his doctrine on the recipient. The word *sacramentum* had meant in Latin (among other things) the oath of allegiance to the officer taken by a recruit to the army. Similarly, said Zwingli, the Sacraments are oaths of allegiance to Christ. But, replies Calvin, this is not the reason why the Church fathers called them 'Sacraments'. Nor does it at all express their nature.

At the other extreme was the scholastic doctrine, carried over from the Middle Ages into the sixteenth century, which ascribed an inherent power to the Sacraments, a power to justify and confer grace, granted that no mortal sin formed an obstacle. In reply Calvin goes to Augustine's distinction between the Sacrament itself and the 'matter' or 'substance' of the Sacrament. The Sacrament is the sign pointing to the *res*, the entity itself. That which belongs to the *res* must not be transferred to the sign. The 'matter' or 'substance' of the Sacraments is Christ himself. Their efficacy consists in 'fostering, confirming and increasing in us the true knowledge of Christ, as well as assisting us to possess him more fully and to enjoy his riches' (xiv.16, 273[22–24]). And this takes place when they are received by faith. Not that their power and truth depend on our faith; they would still be powerful and true if they encountered unbelief, for God's institution stands firm.

Gospel and Sacraments have one end: 'Therefore let it remain fixed that the Sacraments have no other functions than the Word. These are, to offer and set before us Christ, and in him the treasures of heavenly grace' (xiv.17, 274[18-20]).

In Scripture there are two kinds of Sacraments. The first are in natural things, the other in miracles. Examples of the first are the tree of life in the Garden (Gen 2:9, 17) and the rainbow after the Flood (Gen 9:13–14). In each instance a natural thing was used by God to become the instrument of a promise, in fact, a Sacrament. 'Before, the tree was – a tree, the rainbow – a rainbow. But when they were inscribed with the Word of God a new form was imposed on them, so that they began to be what they had not been before' (xiv.18, 276[16-18]). They were like silver made into coins, still silver, but now coins. Examples of the second kind of Sacrament are Gideon's fleece (Judges 6:37) and Hezekiah's sundial (2 Kings 20:9ff.). Both these were miracles, but they were also Sacraments, in that the signs were intended to confirm the faith of Gideon and Hezekiah in the promises God had given them.

In the Church, Sacraments have been various. Under the old Covenant there was circumcision and later the purifications and sacrifices and so on in the Law. After Christ had come the Sacraments were Baptism and the Lord's Supper. That is, looking at the whole Church. Such sacramental acts as the laying-on of hands at ordination, the Sacrament of Orders, cannot be classed with the two Sacraments because they apply only to one part of the Church, in this case the clergy, 'although I am not unwilling to let it be called a Sacrament' (xiv.20, 278[18]). In fact there is no difference between the Sacraments of the Old and New Testaments, except that the former sketch out obscurely the Christ still promised, whereas the latter bear witness to him as already revealed.

(ii) Baptism

Having stated the nature and purpose of the Sacraments in general, it remains for Calvin to apply this in particular to those to which the title of Sacrament may legitimately be given. The first is Baptism, 'the sign of initiation by which we are adopted into the fellowship (*societas*) of the Church, so that, ingrafted in Christ, we may be reckoned among the children of God' (xv.1, 285[12-13]). It is important to notice that 'by which' agrees in the Latin with 'the sign' and not with 'initiation'. The adoption, the ingrafting and the reckoning among God's children are by this sign, Baptism.

It is as the *symbolum* of cleansing, rather than as the Pauline image of death, burial and resurrection (Rom 6:1ff.), that Calvin mainly treats of Baptism; that is, as the complete removing of sin. For Baptism is like a signed document in which God declares that 'all our sins are so blotted out, covered over, consigned to oblivion, that they never come into his sight, are never remembered, never imputed' (xv.1, 285$^{22-24}$). Plainly, therefore, Baptism is the enaction of the primary message of the Gospel, that our sins are forgiven. In it the knowledge and assurance that we are cleansed from sin, regenerate and renewed are received.

But the heart of the matter has still to be shown. To call Baptism a sign or a symbol is meaningless without also saying what is signified and symbolized. That water washes and Baptism symbolizes washing from sin states only the end of the Sacrament. Its real symbolism lies in the cleansing blood of Christ ('the blood of Jesus Christ, his Son, cleanseth us from all sin'; 1 John 1:7). The blood is figured by the water of Baptism. Hence Baptism directs our faith to Christ alone as the Saviour from sin.

We must not forget the first sentence, which spoke of initiation. For Baptism has not only a backward reference, in forgiving the past, but also a future. This is why it is once for all; we are 'washed and cleansed once for the whole of our life' (xv.3, 287$^{6-7}$). When we fall into sin after Baptism what is to be renewed is not our Baptism but the memory of our Baptism. It is not obliterated by subsequent sin, because it is stronger than sin, inasmuch as what is given in it is the purity of Christ, which remains ever alive and triumphant. What lies behind Calvin's insistence here is the place given to Baptism in the mediaeval order of salvation. The grace of Baptism was regarded as forfeited by subsequent sin and needed to be renewed by the Sacrament of penance.

Baptism also demonstrates that in Christ we have died to sin and in him have new life. We are taken back to chapters iii–vii of Book III – Baptism is the external means or aid to effect repentance and regeneration. At this point he turns to Romans 6:3–4, where we learn that by Baptism Christ makes us partakers of his Death and Resurrection: 'we truly feel the efficacy of Christ's death in the mortification of our flesh and at the same time the efficacy of his resurrection in the quickening of the Spirit [our spirit?]' (xv.5, 288$^{32-34}$).

We must go further. In Baptism we are not only partakers of Christ's Death and Resurrection, but of Christ himself and of all the blessings that he possesses. He himself was baptized, and that 'in order that he might have it in common with us, as a most firm bond of the union and society into which he condescended to enter with us' (xv.6, 289[10–12]). And, once again, it is Christ himself who is the 'proper object of Baptism' (xv.6, 289[16]).

The current Romanist doctrine was that Baptism released and freed from the original sin which began with Adam's Fall, and restored to the same righteousness which he possessed before the Fall. Calvin replies that although it is true that 'there is no condemnation to them that are in Christ Jesus' (Rom 8:1), yet the *perversitas* of nature, 'the mind of the flesh' (Rom 8:7), never leaves the believer in this life, but brings forth the works of the flesh. *Concupiscentia*, as we heard earlier, is like a furnace that goes on shooting out sparks and flames, a spring with a never-ceasing flow of water. But Calvin has already said that the power of Christ overcomes sin. The remission of sins in Baptism looks forward as well as backward.

The second purpose in Baptism is dealt with only briefly. It is the open profession that we wish to be reckoned among the people of God, a public witness that we agree in one worship of God and one religion with all Christians.

After the purpose, Calvin turns to the way in which it should be used and received. Above all, he says, we must receive Baptism as if from the hand of its author, Christ, 'being assured that he speaks to us through the sign; that it is he that cleanses us, washes us, and blots out the remembrance of our offences; he that makes us sharers of his death; he that takes away the kingdom from Satan; he that weakens the power of our *concupiscentia*; nay, he that unites in one with us so that, clothed in him, we are accounted children of God' (xv.14, 295[10–16]). The surest rule of the Sacraments is that they are the analogy or similitude that in these bodily things we are to perceive spiritual things as closely as if they were set in front of our eyes. Nor is this an empty spectacle. Christ brings us by faith to what is present. What he figures in the Sacrament he at the same time fulfils efficaciously.

If we receive Baptism as if from the hand of Christ, it follows that its validity is not to be measured by the worthiness of the minister who administers it, as in the early centuries the Donatists, and in the Reformers' days the Anabaptists, taught. The Anabaptists insisted on rebaptism for those who had been baptized by Romanist priests. To them Calvin's reply is that Baptism is not into a particular Church, but into the Faith of Christ. Under the Papacy

Baptism was *in nomine Patris et Filii et Spiritus Sancti*, and the baptizer was not a priest, but Christ.

But, answered the Anabaptists, there was no faith then, or perhaps for several years, to receive the promises. Quite true; we were blind for a long time after we had been baptized. But God's promise is true and stands firm; and when we begin at last to repent, then the truth of our Baptism is realized in us. When we were baptized by a priest we received the promise, later we embraced it by faith.

Having thus considered 'the power, the dignity, and the utility of this mystery' (xv.19, 299[25]), Calvin goes on to speak of the actual administration of the rite. It is a pity that so much has been added – the giving of a candle, the chrism and so forth. Far better to keep to the bare simplicity, so that the symbolism is not obscured by secondary acts with different symbolic meanings. In outlining the preferable shape of the service Calvin is giving the practice in the Genevan Liturgy: 'When anyone is to be baptized, he is to be represented in the assembly of believers and offered to God, with the whole Church as it were witnessing it and praying over him; the Confession of Faith in which the catechumen is to be trained should be recited, the promises which are contained in Baptism are to be related; the catechumen is to be baptized in the name of the Father and of the Son and of the Holy Spirit; and finally he is to be dismissed with prayers and thanksgivings' (xv.19, 300[7–13]).

There is no need for us to follow him through chapter xvi in defence of infant Baptism against the Anabaptists, for it has already become plain that he saw infant Baptism as the norm. As for other details, it is immaterial whether Baptism is by immersion or sprinkling, although the former was the practice in the early Church. The command to baptize was made to the Apostles only, and is therefore the duty of their successors, who have the ministry of the Word and Sacraments. No others may baptize, even in cases where the infant is in danger of death; for it is wrong to think that unbaptized infants must go to hell. God's promises are to believers and their children, even the promise of salvation.

(iii)   The Lord's Supper[5]

We move forward from the Sacrament of regeneration. Chapter xvii, 'On the Holy Supper of the Lord and what it confers on us', begins thus: 'After God has once [i.e., in Baptism] received us into his family, he regards us not only as servants but as his children. To fulfil the offices of a completely good Father he cares for his offspring and undertakes to nourish us continually throughout our lives. And, not content with that, he wishes to make us even more certain of his continued kindness by giving us a pledge' (xvii.1, 342^{3-7}). Just as Christ was the subject of Baptism, so he is also of the Lord's Supper in which he 'testifies that he is the life-giving bread with which our souls are fed unto true and blessed immortality' (xvii.1, 342^{9-11}).

Before discussing the doctrine, Calvin explains his proposed method of working. First he will give a *summa* of the doctrine, making it easy for non-theologians to understand. After that he will go on to unravel the many knots with which Satan has entangled the doctrine. We will be principally concerned with the *summa*, contained in paragraphs 1–11.

The fundamental concept is what the name suggests, a meal by which the regenerate are nourished. The bread and wine are, first of all, signs 'representing to us the invisible food which we receive from the body and blood of Christ' (xvii.1, 342^{20-22}). As a good Father God feeds his children and invites them to partake of Christ, the unique food of their souls. The union of Christ with the believer is a mystery completely beyond our grasp. Therefore, God has supplied us with a figure of it in the Lord's Supper, where the earthly elements are within our comprehension and make us as certain of the reality they represent as if we could actually see it. The dullest mind can understand the similitude that as bread and wine sustain the body, so souls are fed with Christ.

The purpose of this 'mystical blessing' is to confirm to us that the body of Christ was once so sacrificed for us that we now feed on him 'and in feeding feel within ourselves the efficacy of that unique sacrifice' (xvii.1, 343^{8-9}). Similarly, it is confirmed to us that his blood was once so shed that it is the perpetual drink of God's children. Hence the words of promise spoken in the institution of the Lord's Supper, 'Take, eat; this is my body which is given for you' (Matt 26:26 and parallels).

Calvin now speaks, as if from the pulpit, on the significance of the union of Christ and the believer, this 'wonderful interchange' in which what is Christ's becomes the believer's, what is the believer's becomes Christ's. He is the heir of life; therefore the believer is also. The believer is a sinner, but his sin is transferred to Christ, imputed to him and not to the believer. Christ became the Son of man that we might become sons of God, he descended to earth that we might ascend to heaven, he took our mortality that he might give us his immortality; and so on.

The Lord's Supper witnesses to all this as surely as if Christ were present in our sight and able to be touched by our hands. The words of institution, 'This is my body which is given for you; this is my blood which is shed for you', declare that Christ is given to us to be ours. And 'the whole force of the Sacrament' lies in the phrases 'which is given for you', 'which is shed for you'. Calvin returns to the 'sure analogy' that 'as bread nourishes, sustains, and maintains the life of our body, so the body of Christ is the unique food which animates and quickens the soul' (xvii.3, 345[1–3]). Similarly with wine and the blood of Christ.

Yet the chief thing in the Lord's Supper is not the body of Christ *per se*, but the promise that is attached to feeding on his body: 'I am the bread of life; whoever eats of my body shall have everlasting life' (John 6:35, 51). This is to be understood of Christ crucified: 'we do not rightly and savingly feed on Christ except as he is crucified' (xvii.4, 345[20]). It is, therefore, the crucified body, the shed blood, to which the Lord's Supper bears witness; 'it sends us to the Cross' (xvii.4, 345[18]).

All that Christ is and has done for us becomes ours when it is applied to us by the preaching of the Gospel and 'even more clearly by the holy Supper where he offers himself to us with all his blessings and we receive him by faith' (xvii.5, 346[2–4]). It reminds us that Christ became the bread of life and it promises that everything he did and suffered was in order to give us eternal life. He was the bread of life inasmuch as he was born as man and died and rose again, but he would not now be the bread of life except that the efficacy of his Birth, Death and Resurrection is eternal. In his sermons Calvin will sometimes speak of Christ's shed blood never drying, but continuing fresh and living down the ages. 'He once gave [his body] to become bread when he surrendered himself to be crucified for the redemption of the world. He daily gives it for our participation, in that it was crucified, by the word of the Gospel, when he seals that revelation by the holy mystery of the Supper, when he fulfils inwardly what he signifies outwardly' (xvii.5, 346[21–25]).

There are two opposite faults to be avoided. The one is to minimize the signs and thus lose what they signify. The other is to overpraise the signs so that they obscure what they signify. The first was the error of the Zwinglians. They interpreted the Johannine statements about eating the flesh and drinking the blood of Christ

155

figuratively as meaning believing in Christ. For Calvin 'eating' was not faith itself, but the consequence of faith. This is no mere semantics, for 'by declaring that he is the bread of life the Lord wished to teach not only that our salvation rests in faith in his Death and Resurrection, but also that by true communion with him his life passes into us and becomes ours, just as bread when taken as food provides energy to the body' (xvii.5, 347$^{26-30}$).

Nor is the Lord's Supper a purely spiritual communion. This would disregard the elements and also the Johannine promises. But here Calvin confesses his inability to do justice to such a sublime mystery. All his words are mere childishness: 'Nothing is left for me but to burst out in wonder at the mystery of it, which neither the mind is equal to think nor the tongue to explain' (xvii.7, 349$^{20-23}$). Nevertheless, he will set out in summary form his judgement on the Lutheran doctrine of the ubiquity of Christ's flesh, which is the point at issue here.[6] Later he will deal with the subject more fully in paragraphs 16ff.

Scripture bears witness to Christ as from the beginning the life-giving Word of the Father and the fountain of life. When he became man and took flesh, that life was manifested. But man, for whom he came, had fallen into death. What good would it do man to behold life afar off in a Word remote from him? By taking flesh, however, the Word is no longer far and hidden, but reveals himself so as to be partaken. He makes the flesh in which he dwells to be life-giving to us so that we may feed by participation with him, unto immortality. For he is not life only as the eternal Word, but diffuses his power into the flesh he took so that the communion of life might flow to us. In itself his flesh was mortal and, therefore, not life-giving. Its immortality and virtue of giving life are from his Divinity. Then 'the flesh of Christ is like a rich and inexhaustible fountain which transfuses into us the life flowing into itself from the Divinity' (xvii.9, 350^{38}–351^2). This concept, so vital for Calvin's doctrine of the Lord's Supper, is called the *caro vivifica Christi*, 'the life-giving flesh of Christ'.

And so Calvin sums up his positive doctrine of the Lord's Supper. Souls are fed by the flesh and blood of Christ just as bread and wine feed the body. This can only be because he becomes one with us and refreshes us by the eating his flesh and drinking his blood. But how can this be? By the secret power of the Holy Spirit who 'truly unites things locally disjoined' (xvii.10, 351^{31}). This is testified and sealed in the Lord's Supper, not by an empty sign pointing away from itself to a remote entity, but 'by the Spirit there exerting his efficacy, by which he fulfils what he promises' (xvii.10, 351$^{35-36}$). Certainly, these are symbolic actions; but God does not set before us empty symbols. What is enacted symbolically is truly present and revealed: 'For why does the Lord put in your hand the symbol of his body, except that he may assure you of true participation with him?' (xvii.10, 352$^{18-20}$). He closes this part of the chapter by repeating what he had said earlier and by putting his *summa* into Aristotelian terms. The Lord's Supper consists of the corporeal signs of bread and wine and the invisible reality which is figured and revealed by the symbols. The Sacrament can be understood in three parts: its signification, in that it points to the promises; its 'matter', which is Christ with his Death and Resurrection; and its effects, that is, redemption, righteousness, sanctification, and life.

I say, therefore, that in the mystery of the Supper Christ, and, what is more, his body and blood in which he fulfilled all obedience to procure righteousness for us, is truly revealed to us through the symbols of bread and wine, by which we coalesce into one body with him and then are made partakers of his substance and feel his power by participation in all his blessings. (xvii.11, 354$^{19-25}$)

5 CIVIL GOVERNMENT[7]

From the mountain heights where our author has been adoring the sacramental mystery that passes his understanding we descend to the mundane plains of politics and civil life. This climatic shock has proved too much for some writers. Wendel,[8] wishing no doubt to end on a lofty note, transferred politics to an earlier chapter. Yet Calvin had sound historical and theological reasons for his course. He has already, he reminds us, shown that man is under a twofold rule, the one relating to his soul, 'the other which belongs only to the regulation of civil and external moral righteousness' (xx.1, 471$^{15-16}$). Although it seems remote from 'the spiritual teaching of faith', Calvin is compelled to undertake it here, partly because of the revolutionary and even anarchistic tendencies of some Anabaptist groups, partly because of, at the other extreme, the fearful king-worship in the sixteenth century, of which Machiavelli was the most famous, but by no means only, exponent. But there is also the theological necessity; and this it is that unites the chapter with the rest of the *Institutio* and also rounds off the whole work. Civil government is a gift of God, that we may know how kindly he looks after the human race and that 'a zeal for *pietas* may be the more vigorous in us to testify our gratitude' (xx.1, 472$^{1-3}$). This is the language of the early chapters of the *Institutio* – 'to know', 'God's kindness', '*pietas*', 'gratitude'. And that politics is for Calvin a matter of faith is shown when he says that unless the anarchism and king-worship are checked, 'the soundness of the Faith will perish' (xx.1, 471$^{24-25}$).

First Calvin turns against the Anabaptists. They have misunderstood the meaning of the promises about Christian liberty and the equality of all in Christ Jesus. Consequently, they think that they do not enjoy liberty while there are rulers and judges and laws. But they are confusing two régimes, the spiritual kingdom of Christ and civil organization. These are not mutually destructive opposites, for 'spiritual liberty can stand perfectly well with political servitude' (xx.1, 472$^{25-26}$), and Christ's kingdom is not a matter of nationality, social status, or degree of civilization.

Another tendency in Anabaptism was to regard the earthly régime as below the Christian, who is dead from the elements of the world, as Paul taught, and has been translated into God's kingdom and is with Christ in the heavenly. Although, replies Calvin, the two régimes are distinct they are not contradictory. The heavenly kingdom begins in us while we are still on earth. We aspire towards our genuine fatherland, but meanwhile we are pilgrims in the world. It is precisely as pilgrims that we need such helps as political order. By calling this sphere a 'help', he recalls us to the title of the Book. Political order, then, is (like the Church and the Sacraments) one of the 'outward Means or Helps by which God invites us into the Society of Christ and keeps us in it'. Perhaps the plain is not so far below the mountain heights after all. This is certainly true when Calvin explains the purpose of the earthly régime as 'to cherish and protect the outward service of God, to defend the sound teaching of *pietas* and the condition of the Church, to regulate our lives for human society, to form our morals for civil justice, to reconcile us one with another, to nurse the common peace and tranquillity' (xx.2, 473$^{12-17}$). Believers are human beings and those who take away their earthly helps 'tear off their humanity' (xx.2, 473$^{21-22}$). Political order is as necessary as bread, water, sun, or air; more necessary, in fact, for it is not only concerned with these earthly needs, but has also the duty of putting down idolatry and irreligion and of maintaining such a public order that every man may live in safety and may have innocent intercourse with others, and that decency and modesty may flourish.

Calvin maps out the route he intends to take. First he will consider the function of the ruler, whether this is a lawful calling which God approves; in what its office consists; and what power it possesses. Secondly, by what laws the Christian state should be governed. And thirdly, the use of those laws by the people themselves and their obedience to the ruler.

It was not difficult for Calvin to demonstrate from Scripture that the office of ruler is approved by God. It is from God that he has his mandate to rule. He is, therefore, endowed with God's authority and acts as his representative and in his place. It is 'a calling not only holy and lawful in God's sight, but also the most sacred and by far the most honourable in the whole life of mortals' (xx.4, 475^{29-31}).

As to which of the three forms of government is preferable, monarchy, aristocracy, or democracy, Calvin will not speak too firmly. They all have their dangers; monarchy can degenerate into dictatorship, aristocracy into powerful cliques, democracy into anarchy. All in all, Calvin prefers aristocracy, or aristocracy tempered with democracy, on the ground that it presents less danger than the others. Nevertheless, there are various forms of government in the world and each state must adopt that which suits it best.

Calvin is less concerned with divine right than with the divine duty of kings. The ruler's duty is summed up in the Ten Commandments, just like any other person's. His first duty is the care of *pietas* as it is set out in the first Table of the Commandments. The second Table shows that it is for him to create the conditions in which men may live with their fellows and also to put these last six Commandments into effect in his own territories. The Sixth Commandment raises the question of capital punishment and war. Calvin asserts that governments have the right to punish some crimes by death and also to wage war, so long as it is 'just'. There is also the problem of whether, in view of the Commandment 'Thou shalt not steal', governments have a right to levy taxes.

Secondly, by what laws a state should be governed. In disagreeing that a modern state should be ruled by the Mosaic Law, Calvin was giving only half of his opinion. The Mosaic Law is to be divided into the three parts of moral, ceremonial and judicial. The first applies to all men always and everywhere, since it commands them 'to worship God with pure faith and *pietas* and to embrace [others] in a sincere love' (xx.15, 487[4–5]). The ceremonial laws applied only to the Jews, to foreshadow Christ until he should come. The judicial laws were 'sure forms of equity and justice, by which [the people] might behave innocently and quietly among themselves' (xx.15, 487[15–17]). Because Christ has come, the ceremonial laws are abrogated. The judicial laws were fitted to the conditions under which the people of old lived, not to modern conditions. Only the moral laws are still operative. It is therefore plain that the Mosaic Law is not binding on modern states. They are free to frame their own laws according to local or national needs. But the proviso must be added that these modern laws must be consonant with the comprehensive moral laws in the Mosaic Law.

Thirdly, what is the use for the 'general society of Christians' of the civil régime, composed of rulers, laws, and courts? Moreover, to what extent should private persons defer to rulers? How far should their civil obedience go?

The first area Calvin considers here is the Christian's use of law for settling disputes. There are those who regard all litigation as unChristian. But, says Calvin, according to Paul, the ruler (here the judicial system) is a minister of God for your good (Rom 13:4). Therefore, Christians may legitimately use the law courts, though without being litigious. They should be clear about their motives. If it is a question of the best way to settle a dispute, well and good. But there should be no spirit of hatred or revenge. Indeed, the adversary should be treated with love and goodwill. As a lawyer Calvin was aware that this could be regarded as so idealistic as to be unreal. Because it is rare, however, it is no less true. Calvin goes on to reconcile his position with Jesus' teaching in the Sermon on the Mount (Matt 5:39ff.) and Paul's in 1 Corinthians 6:5–8. Whether he was altogether successful in this, the point to be remembered is that he regarded civil law as one of the helps for Christians in their pilgrimage.

Deference to rulers was an easier matter. Subjects, like rulers, have a divine duty; in this case to obey. Obedience should extend to all rulers, whether good or bad. It is to the office, not to the holder of the office, that deference is due. Similarly, the obedience of the subject extends to lawful commands of various sorts, to paying taxes, and so on. Disobedience to the ruler and his commands is in fact disobedience to God, whose vicegerent the ruler is. Nor, when he dislikes the demands or considers them unlawful, may he take the law into his own hands. He must seek redress by constitutional means.

But it is the bad ruler who occupies Calvin for most of the rest of this chapter. He insists in paragraph after paragraph that, however unworthy the ruler, his subjects are still to revere the office he represents. This is not merely a matter of convenience but a part of *pietas*. Despite the almost universal dislike of 'kings' that he expressed so frequently throughout his writings, he continued to insist on reverence for the office of ruler.

We are brought to the question of the legitimacy of disobedience and even rebellion. If such reverence is to be shown to rulers, however worthless or tyrannical, is no check to be placed on them? Calvin did not swerve from his fundamental position, even under very strong pressure from the persecuted French Protestants a year or two after the final *Institutio* was published. It was not for private persons to throw off the yoke and rebel. The only check lay with constitutionally appointed bodies, who had the duty of interfering in order to save the state or to ameliorate the condition of the people. Calvin cites three examples in classical times from Sparta, Rome and Athens, and continues: 'as things are now [these duties] are performed in individual states by the three "orders", when they exercise their chief assemblies. So far am I from forbidding them to do their duty in interfering with the wild licence of kings that I affirm that their dissimulation is a wicked treachery if they weakly connive at kings using violence and trampling down the humble people' (xx.31, 501$^{20-26}$). The three 'orders' he meant were the three 'estates' in France of nobles, clergy, and burgesses. At the time he was writing they had not sat for many years. How far this politically important paragraph (31) is meant to be taken is a matter of debate. For our present purpose we need only point to the two principles that the duty of private persons is to obey the ruler, and that therefore they do not have the right to rebel, and that it is the duty of the constitutionally appointed bodies to exercise their duty of being at the least a check on the ruler and presumably going as far as the particular circumstances demand.

It is with the thought of obeying God rather than men that the *Institutio*, perhaps somewhat abruptly, closes. With *pietas* the work has begun; on the same note it ends: 'And lest we should faint Paul applies another spur, "we were redeemed by Christ at such a price as our redemption cost him, in order not to be slaves to the depraved desires of men", far less should we be bound to *impietas*' (xx.32, 502$^{27-31}$).

Notes

1 See K. McDonnell, *John Calvin, the Church, and the Eucharist* (Princeton, 1967).

2 *The Register of the Company of Pastors of Geneva in the Time of Calvin*, ed. and tr. P. E. Hughes (Grand Rapids, 1966), p. 41.

3 CO 11, 41.

4 See R. S. Wallace, *Calvin's Doctrine of the Word and Sacraments* (Edinburgh, 1953).

5 See K. McDonnell, op. cit.; J. W. Nevin, *The Mystical Presence* (1846; repr. Philadelphia, 1966).

6 Luther taught that inasmuch as Christ's risen body was glorified it was no longer subject to conditions of space – i.e., it was ubiquitous. Therefore, it was present both in heaven and also under the forms of bread and wine. See E. G. Rupp and B. Drewery (eds), *Martin Luther* (London, 1970), pp. 132–5.

7 See E. Chenevière, *La pensée politique de Calvin* (Geneva, 1970); R. M. Kingdon and R. D. Linders (eds), *Calvin and Calvinism: Sources of Democracy?* (Lexington, 1970).

8 F. Wendel, *Calvin: The Origins and Development of His Religious Thought* (London, 1963).

Index

Printed in the United States
703400006B